OPENMIND/
WHOLEMIND

OPENMIND/ WHOLEMIND

PARENTING AND TEACHING TOMORROW'S CHILDREN TODAY

by Bob Samples

Jalmar Press

Rolling Hills Estates, California

Photos and Drawings: Bob Samples.
Layout and Design: Bob Samples, Cheryl Charles and Stician Marin Samples.
Editing: Suzanne Mikesell and Cheryl Charles.
Word Processing for Typeset Telecommunication: Judy Dawson and Cheryl Charles.
Telecommunications: Graphic Directions; Linda Brown.
Printing: Lithographic Press; Don Caven, Project Manager.
Publisher: Jalmar Press; Brad Winch, President.
4MAT is a registered trademark of Excel Incorporated and Bernice McCarthy.

Library of Congress Cataloging-in-Publication Data

Samples, Bob.
Openmind/Wholemind: Parenting and Teaching Tomorrow's Children Today.

1. Child development. 2. Child psychology. 3. Learning. 4. Home and school. I. Title. II. Title: Openmind/Wholemind.
LB1115.S24 1986   155.4'13 86-27566
ISBN 0-915190-45-1

Published by Jalmar Press
45 Hitching Post Drive, Building 2
Rolling Hills Estates, California 90274

First U.S. Printing   ISBN 0-915190-45-1

R. Buckminster Fuller

For two honored teachers

Stician Marin Samples

Foreword

As our society transforms from an industrial to a post-industrial structure, it will be necessary to reinvent many of our most important institutions. Included in this process of recreation will be our arrangements for work, government and politics, for international relations, commerce and economics, play and leisure, and for parenting and nurturing the young. In fact, this last item is likely the most important, because through the process of nurturing we are preparing the navigators of the ship of the future. They will have to guide the planet through times rich in opportunity, but also rich in danger and challenge. We will need a full measure of our most vital natural resources—human creativity, patience, courage, imagination, and empathy. But many of our traditional arrangements for nurturing the young, especially schooling, parenting, and the family, were created or shaped in their current form for an industrial era now fast disappearing. We need a guide, a concept plan, or a vision of how we might reshape them to more appropriate forms. Few people are better able to provide such a set of ideas than Bob Samples.

Bob has explored the dimensions of human development and the nurturing of human capacities in many books and articles over the past two decades. He was among the first educators to recognize the potential implications of brain research to schooling. He has consistently urged us to reconsider the cultural limitations that we have imposed on our definition of human talents and capacities. *OPENMIND/WHOLEMIND* is an important extension of his ideas inviting parents and teachers alike to redesign their traditional approaches to supporting and promoting the growth and development of young people. Perhaps as important, through the process of transforming our metaphors for educating and parenting, we also have an opportunity to reinvent the personal metaphors through which we think about our own growth and empowerment. *OPENMIND/WHOLEMIND* will be an important asset for those wishing to move ahead into a new world, one which is safer and healthier at personal, community, and planetary levels.

Milton McClaren, Ph.D.,Professor, Faculty of Science and Faculty of Education, Simon Fraser University

Foreword

OPENMIND/WHOLEMIND is both an inspiring and a practical book. It offers a vision of the future, and a way to make the present more rich and fulfilled.

OPENMIND/WHOLEMIND is for parents. It is for parents of infants, toddlers, small children, emerging adolescents, full-fledged teenagers, and blossoming adults.

OPENMIND/WHOLEMIND is for teachers—teachers of youth from nurseries and day care centers, preschools, elementary and secondary schools, and adult learning programs.

OPENMIND/WHOLEMIND is for anyone who is genuinely interested in nurturing, supporting, and extending the capacities of others.

OPENMIND/WHOLEMIND is for anyone who is fascinated and challenged by the potential to learn, grow, and change in each individual human being—including one's self.

In this book, the reader will find a variety of helpful information and ideas. Bob Samples is uniquely capable of synthesizing concepts from the fields of psychology, education, natural science, and business. He does so with a clarity and elegance that transforms the complex to the understandable.

In addition to the book's solid foundation on principles of teaching and learning, the book includes a remarkable and refreshing set of specific suggestions for real things each of us can do in our own lives in order to be more balanced, fulfilled, healthy, creative, and constructive.

OPENMIND/WHOLEMIND is honest. It is based on the insights and actual experiences of the author. I know the ideas, strategies, and recommendations that Bob Samples offers in this book will and do actually work. I know this as a teacher who works with learners of all ages, designing and directing educational programs in the United States and Canada. These programs are aimed at creating a balance between natural and cultural systems for a healthy and sustainable future—in our own lives, at a personal level, and throughout the planet.

I also know *OPENMIND/WHOLEMIND* to be honest and effective from my unique vantage as Bob Samples' partner, wife, and mother of our son, Stician. It has been my privilege to learn with Bob—as well as with Stician. This book is a statement to our son's integrity and vision, as much as our commitment and concern. It is a chronicle of laughter, learning, frustration, and hope. It is a statement to our shared belief in the power of the present and the promise of the future.

Cheryl Charles, Ph.D.
Parent, Educator, Author

Table of Contents

Part V
Episodes, Reflections and Explorations

Part VI
The Edges of Knowing

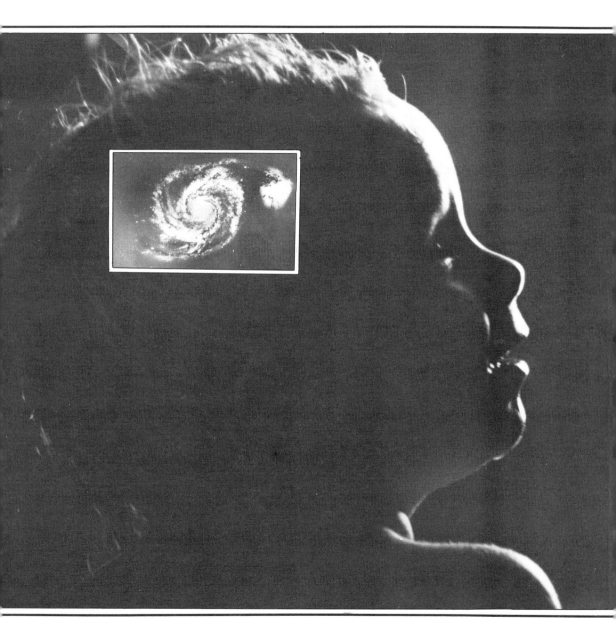

MIND: THE INFINITE CONTEXT

PART I

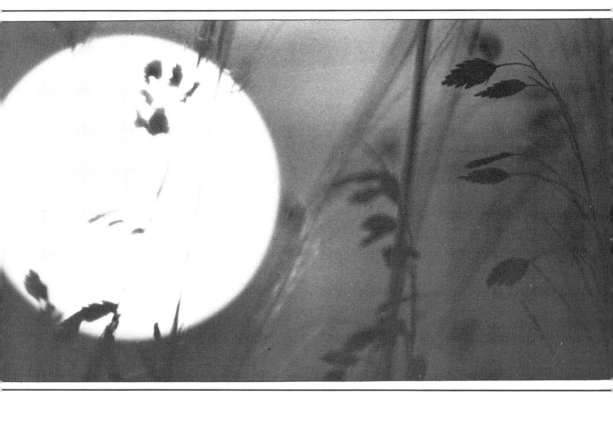

Beginnings: A Summer to Learn

After a particularly frustrating session with a class of eight-year-olds, a group of us who were writing instructional materials retired to lick our wounds. More precisely, we retired to minister to *my* wounds. Our strategy for several days had been to designate one of us as "teacher" and the others as observers who made notes on how well the lesson was taught. I was the educational novice of the four-member team and I had conceived that day's lesson.

I knew I had done poorly. The main points of the lesson had escaped the children in spite of my insistence that they "get the message." I could tell that my colleagues hadn't missed a thing, as they sat busily chatting about everything but my disastrous performance. Finally, I interrupted the small talk, exclaiming, "I don't know what went wrong! They kept getting the wrong answer!"

Silence. The silence spoke clearly that each of my colleagues had experienced similar anguish. I stood helplessly, hoping that someone could tell me how to avoid feeling such frustration again. Then, the senior team member spoke. He was Jerome Bruner, a psychologist at Harvard. "Wrong answer?" His voice was deeply resonant and filled with warmth. He repeated, "Wrong answer?" He looked fully at me and said, "Bob, children never give you a wrong answer, they just answer a different question. And the answer they give you is the correct answer to that different question."

Bruner then said, "Bob it is our responsibility to find out what question the child answered correctly—we have to honor what the child *knows* as well as what we *want* the child to know."

3

That advice was given me some twenty years ago and its impact has stayed with me to this day. The members of that team gave generously and unhesitatingly of themselves, and each was vital to the thinking that guided my life and work for the next two decades. One was Richard Jones, then a colleague of Abraham Maslow at Brandeis University. Richard was committed to understanding the roles of fantasy and feeling in education. Another team member was Margaret Donaldson, at that time a faculty member at the University of Edinburgh. She also studied fantasy, emotions and the role of night dreaming in the educational process. Another occasional team member was Eleanor Duckworth, a graduate student of Bruner's at Harvard University's Center for Cognitive Studies. Eleanor left shortly thereafter to study in Geneva with Jean Piaget.

In the years that have followed, I have been privileged to explore the nature of teaching and learning and the growth of knowledge in children and adults. I have become increasingly convinced that, as children learn, they do many more things than we commonly give them credit for. I have also become certain that what Jones and Donaldson defended in the realms of fantasy, dreaming and feelings is not peripheral but central to the acquisition of knowledge. By ignoring these and emphasizing rationality and logic, our culture has chosen to define learning and intelligence in amazingly limited ways.

Human nature is a spirit living in time and space. Edith Cobb

OPENMIND/WHOLEMIND is the result of a three-decade quest into how the human brain-mind system works. It is an exploration of the miraculous acts of thinking, learning and knowing. You will notice I hyphenate brain-mind. I do so to emphasize the unity I feel they represent. Were it not so cumbersome, I would have added a second hyphen to encompass a third word: body. Brain-mind-body: It is vital to consider this trinity as a single entity.

This book represents the most recent phase of my work, a synthesis of brain-mind research as it pertains to learning. This synthesis embraces the interrelationships between Modalities, Intelligences, Learning Styles and Creativity (M.I.S.C.).

M.I.S.C. serves the open mind. It is an approach rich in the contributions of an array of disciplines, of an ever-growing list of scholar-artists of mind. Jerome Bruner, Richard Jones, Gregory Bateson, Buckminster Fuller, Margaret Mead, Mary Budd Rowe and many others have been and are spokespersons for wholeness and unity. Parts I, II, III and IV of *OPEN-MIND/WHOLEMIND* provide background and theoretical perspectives on wholeness and openness, including a discussion of the prevailing models of mind. Parts V and VI provide practical applications and examples directed at parenting and teaching as well as a visit to the realm of possibilities, containing exciting methods for encouraging openness and whole-mindedness in the future.

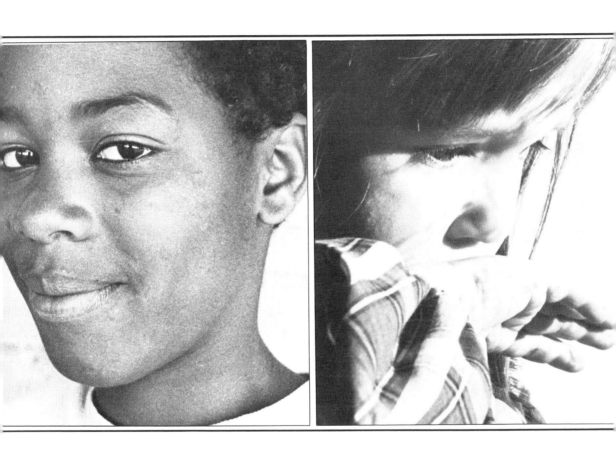

6

The Breadth of Mind

She was afraid. It was the first time she remembered anything like this happening to her. The six-year-old was standing in a room that she sensed having been in before, but she chilled. It was impossible. She had never before been in this city. Her hands were clenched and a shiver of nausea passed through her. Slowly she turned her head toward the gauzed undercurtains that covered the motel window. They tugged at her. She knew when she went to the window she would see, three floors below, a brilliant blue swimming pool with bright beach umbrellas clustered at one end. An eternity seemed to pass as she took the few steps to the window and drew the curtains back. The girl gasped with knowing disbelief, and felt the darkening cloak of fainting begin to close around the edges of her eyes. Only the sound of her mother's voice snatched her back from the edge of unconsciousness. "Isn't this a lovely room? We are so lucky that we could come on this trip."

The boy walked into the living room and said, "Mom, I discovered by myself how easy the nine-times-tables are." Before the woman could respond, the boy excitedly went on, "Whenever you nine-times a number the answer adds up to nine." The woman kneeled to the eight-year-old's eye level and said, "I don't know what you mean, love." "Well . . .," the boy continued, "One times 9 is 9 and 9 by itself is 9. Two times 9 is 18. If you add the 1 and the 8 together it gives you 9. With 9 times 3 you get 27. Two and 7 add up to 9. That's how you check." The mother smiled and said, "I never learned *that* in school." The boy grinned but then seriously added, "I am going to check what happens once you get past 9 times 11. It looks like my rule might change then."

These two children, while seeming to experience remarkably different events, were in fact just exploring different facets of their awesome brain-mind system. The first child, although frightened and bewildered, experienced a facet of mind as normal as that of the budding mathematician. Both his recognition of the pattern in a system of numbers and her capacity to know something before she actually experienced it are design features of the human brain-mind. The effects of these two forms of knowing are worlds apart. The young girl, bathed in fear and disbelief, nearly lost consciousness. The boy felt no such apprehension. Instead, he basked in the glow of confidence and discovery. How can both these be normal?

My search for an answer to this question has been going on for more than two decades. The path has often been obscure but at other times bright and clear. It has led from personal experience to the laboratories of the neurosciences; from classrooms to research in self esteem, self image and the locus of control. These topics often tumbled in chaos but now a settling seems to be at hand. Scholars' ideas in many fields are converging and a comforting clarity about the breadth and depth of mind is emerging.

Part of that emergent unity comes from admitting that the brain-mind system works in ways we once refused to acknowledge. The brain-mind appears to function as an open, self-regulating system. We have lost forever the impoverished mind-as-muscle and mind-as-file-cabinet metaphors that have prevailed for the past several decades. Also gone are the circuit-board models. Even the model of the mind as a computer is a deficit metaphor. Instead we are realizing that the brain-mind functions more as a resonating, self-modifying, holographic, ever-evolving eddy in the open design of the universe.

Freed from the archaic models of yesterday, we stand as beneficiaries of this new image of mind. Aspects of mindwork once thought unique, rare or even deviant are now seen to be part of the grand design, a design sculptured by millions of years of evolution. Rational thought is a gift of that journey but so too are insight, intuition and spontaneous understanding. Reason is a powerful tool but it owes its being to the mystical, mythic dimensions of mind that lie in an aesthetic beyond the parameters of logic.

In these pages we will explore both the overview of the brain-mind system which allows such claims to be made and the application of these findings to parenting and teaching. We each possess a kind of grace in mindwork. We can become more active and proficient in intentionally honoring our own as well as our childrens' capacities and potentials. In the process we can become more creative, more competent and more fulfilled.

A note before going on . . .

I use the words *grace* and *honoring* throughout this book. My own intro-duction to these words came from time spent with native people of North America. *Grace* characterizes a sense of harmony, a sense of fit. It involves a blending of subtle nuances of thought with the vividly obvious. Without *grace*, thought is wooden and mechanistic. The brain-mind is cast as a servant to verifiable orderliness, missing the edges of our immense evolutionary journey. Graceful ideas are those displaying a unique constellation of artistic and scientific qualities.

Albert Einstein was once reported to have said to a colleague that though his equations were correct he couldn't hold much hope for them. The younger man was bewildered. "What is wrong with them?" he protested. Einstein said, "Ideas need more than accuracy, they need grace. These equations are ugly!"

To *honor* is to treat seriously, to attend to. Often, we *know* our mind is doing something or can do something that is totally beyond reason. When we cannot explain or understand how we know this thing, we often ignore or dismiss it—it fades into our unconscious. We dis-honor it. I use *honoring*, then, to invoke the courage and integrity that invites us to accept what we do not yet understand. It is an invitation to go beyond what is understood and believed to what is intrinsically *known*.

A morning needs to be sung to. A new day needs to be honored.
Byrd Baylor

The Native Americans tend to honor all ways of knowing. Native people respect *knowing* as a universal experience, an organic part of nature. *Understanding*, on the other hand, is culture-specific, derived from par-ticular cultural experiences. *We can understand reason but we cannot understand mythic or mystical consciousness*. Yet within us is a power-ful urge to acknowledge our natural ability to apprehend through intui-tion and mythic knowing. To continue with our *knowing* in spite of not *understanding* is an expression of *honoring* our brain-mind design.

Work, Play and Learning

Imbedded in the Graeco-Roman, Judeo-Christian ethic are the tenets that work is necessary, serious and difficult and that play is unnecessary, frivolous and easy. Play is considered *fun* and learning is considered *work*. Accompanying this "truth" is the notion that home is where children play and school is where they work. Play as an idea related to learning thus tends to get bad press. Parents are not acknowledged for the remarkable learnings they guide, teachers are stripped of their instincts to honor the joyous side of learning and play is demeaned as a powerful source of genuine learning. Given such biases, it is little wonder that so much of education has been misunderstood. Yet Bruner and Donaldson demonstrated in their studies that some of life's most significant learnings are acquired in early childhood. Moreover these learnings are *mostly* accomplished in the realm of experience we call play.

How do children learn to walk and talk? Walking is a frightening thing to learn, for in reality *walking is controlled falling*. There are muscles to control and balance to be achieved. It begins with the first attempts to raise a tiny head off the crib mattress. In rapid succession the child kneels, creeps, crawls and finally balances from four- to three- to two-point stabilization. The number of skills involved is overwhelming. Kinesthetic wisdom is involved. So are skills in the affective or feeling and emotional areas. In the brain there is a wildfire of activity. Both cortex areas, the limbic system, the cerebellum and the brain stem all are excited by messages streaming upward from the body. Studies indicate that the bases for later success in thought and reason are established in this motor development stage. If a step is left out, such as creeping, neurological connections in the expanding brain-mind are limited. In later years, problems may emerge in speech, reading and other forms of logical thought.

Many adults forget that walking means the child must abandon his or her hard-earned stability of standing erect. Walking results only when the child learns to orchestrate falling forward with a suite of compensating body movements.

Speech is even more mystifying. Out of gurgling, rolling, lolling sounds, coherent speech emerges. As children are playing with sounds, they are beginning to seek structure and pattern in adult noises. How children recognize the order, pattern and sequencing of sound is still a fundamental mystery to all who have studied the phenomenon. Many scholars are convinced that the structure of language is a powerful determinant of world view. How sound and language pattern the mind and how the mind patterns sound and language remain unknown.

Those who study child development sense that young children possess more ways of knowing than observers can describe. A sad part of "growing up" is that we reduce the number of acceptable ways of experiencing life. Infants show no such discrimination. They treat all experience as appropriate input and heed all their senses at once. With age we become less inclined to attend to the wide variety of stimuli available to us.

As shown in the table below, current research suggests that we are not limited to the traditional five senses. Some researchers are convinced that humans possess many more senses. For example, iron-rich molecules have been detected in human faceplate bones of the sinus cavities. These molecules appear related to our ability to sense the earth's magnetic field and they thus provide an innate sense of direction.

Table of Senses [1]

Sight	Visible Light
Hearing	Vibrations in Air
Touch	Tactile Contact
Taste	Chemical Molecular
Smell	Olfactory-Molecular
Balance-Movement	Kinesthetic Geotropic
Vestibular	Repetitious Movement
Temperature	Molecular Motion
Pain	Nociception
Eidetic Imagery	Neuroelectrical Image Retention
Magnetic	Ferromagnetic Orientation
Infrared	Long Electromagnetic Waves
Ultraviolet	Short Electromagnetic Waves
Ionic	Airborne Ionic Charge
Vomeronasal	Pheromonic Sensing
Proximal	Physical Closeness
Electrical	Surface Charge
Barometric	Atmospheric Pressure
Geogravimetric	Sensing Mass Differences

To emphasize a point, it may well be that infants, not yet knowing which senses are considered "appropriate," will joyfully use them all until they are taught to respond to life using the narrow range acceptable to society. If they do not give up these senses they may be destined for trouble. Adults who don't are frequently labelled deviant. They may be paranormal. They are classified as psychics, seers, aura readers and any of a number of pejorative labels.

The child's enjoyment of the richness of this multisensory world is short-lived for, once he or she learns to walk and talk, the teaching process begins to dominate. The first thing a child learns about walking is that it is dangerous. Safety concerns immediately limit the child's experiences. Things adults consider valuable and harmful are "put up" and out of sight; "safe" things such as toys and household objects that offer little real stimulation are left in place. Perhaps toddlers first learn to distinguish between "serious" things and play at this stage.

A word spoken by chance might have strange consequences. It would suddenly come alive and what people wanted to happen could happen. Nalungiaq

Speech codifies the process. If adult reactions to the child's walking teach what is safe and what is not, adult reactions to speech teach the child what is important and what is not. As rich a gift as speech is, it edits reality. Speech precludes a great deal of direct experience with the world. Many children learn the word "hot" early in life to prevent them from being burned. "Hot" and other words of warning that follow become substitutes for experiences we choose not to let children have. There are times such intervention and caution are appropriate; however, it is likely in many instances that we adults over-correct.

The "play" that previously guided children through learning about the risks of controlled falling and the orchestration of formless sound into speech is turned into a worklike kind of efficiency. *Play* gives way to rules of conduct and codes of conformity defined by culture. Children begin to realize that the sense they made within themselves is not as important as the sense made by others. They are embarking on a strange journey in which their worth will be judged by how willingly and how rapidly they learn cultural rules and submit to existing social structures. If they submit quickly and willingly, they may be called cooperative and intelligent. If not, they may have lives filled with frustration and difficulty.

School institutionalizes the world of "outside sense," the sense of the culture, rather than the inside sense of the child. In school, play makes far less sense than work. Thus school orients its offerings in the form of work and the seriousness it embodies. In our culture, "work" is traditionally a concept not defined or discussed yet characterized by seriousness, appropriateness and obligation. Work results in "right" answers—"right" in the sense of the answers I sought twenty years ago from the group of eight-year-olds.

14

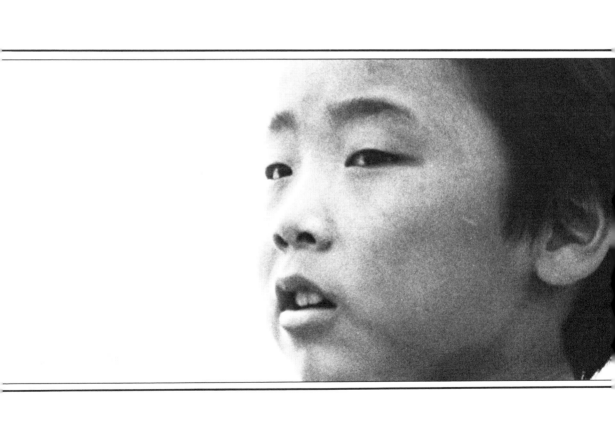

My role as a teacher was to get the right answer from the students. If I did not get the right answer, I was taught to assess the experience in terms of what was wrong with the students. My training had me further limit the students' options until they knew exactly what I wanted. Their job was to provide me with the " right " answer—an answer that fit with "outside" knowledge. In other words, I would make them *work*. Bruner's playful and poignant suggestion forced me to look for the students' "inside" sense—and that perception turned the act of teaching itself into play.

In my life, "play" has grown to embrace the idea of "joyful work." Adults who characterize their work as interesting, worthwhile and joyful employ the word *play* in their descriptions. This is a *play* of integrity, of usefulness and of low exploitation.

Our society seems to be moving toward a merger of these concepts. Enthusiastic, creative, compassionate, cooperative and peaceful are becoming the descriptors of the "new workplace." Dozens of books use similar words to depict future medical and corporate environments and management goals.

It is time to honor the far-ranging attributes of the brain-mind system within the worlds of parenting and teaching. Parenting is the most intimate of teaching settings.

Likewise the goal of teaching must be more than the learner's acquisition of the basics. In schools we must extend compassion, cooperation, commitment and creativity beyond those graces begun in parenting. Learners of all ages must be allowed to use all the capabilities and capacities of our brain-mind design.

Thus, in the pages that follow, expect us to explore how the brain-mind system acquires and expresses experience. Seek with us how the brain-mind system internalizes and processes that experience. We will question and offer alternatives to archaic teaching and parenting rituals that limit experience and close minds.

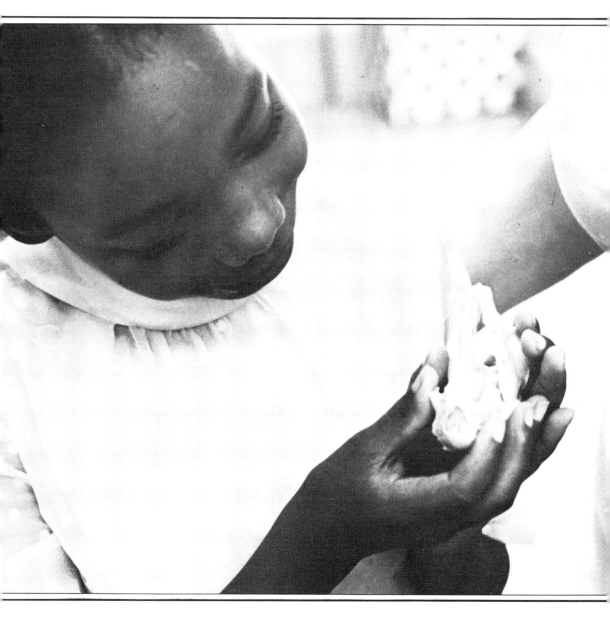

Had I chosen in my teaching to further close the minds of children around the "right" answer, I would not have written a book embracing the commitment of Bruner, Jones and Donaldson. Instead I would have followed the lead of B.F. Skinner and the behaviorists who have established the mainstream of psychological thought. Had I followed them, I would consider the child an integer in a science of manipulation and modification. Children of this vision would get the "right" answers because the answers would be predetermined.

Today, "right" answers seem strange and out of place in a world where certainty is a rare commodity. Futurists are tentative in predicting even the most fundamental changes. Rather than predict, most are satisfied to cite tendencies or trends. The certainty of history has abandoned us to winds of change which bring qualities of social evolution we cannot predict or control.

Men of marble look at me without moving. God help us, child, what have they done to you?
Goethe 1783

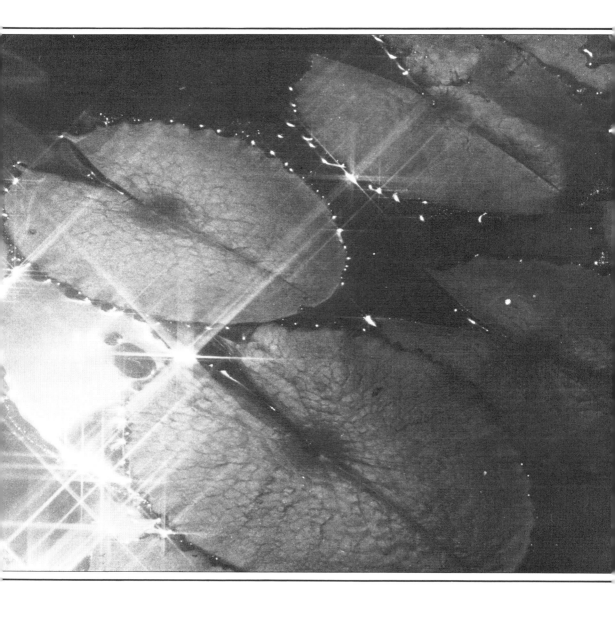

The schools of the future will emerge from these winds of change. They will be different from today's schools, for the requirements of both parenting and schooling will have changed. Our primary focus will be preparing children to cope with what we *do not* know rather than what we *do* know.

It is almost as if schools must re-examine themselves with the goal of developing those conditions of daring experienced by the child learning to walk and speak. Schools must seek, not to re-establish the nineteenth century skills which served an industrial society, but to address the emerging needs of an information age. Our very presence here affirms that we are meant to survive. Our brain, mind and body have served us well. But we also have created self-imposed limitations which are likely to impair our abilities to survive with grace, peace and health in the future.

Now we stand in the dawning light of choices. Our natural design is solid. Our cultural responses have been limiting. The centuries-old pattern of controlling and confirming information is eroding. Our society has created the global village. Television, computers, satellites, space travel and media have filled our consciousness with innumerable options to experience the interconnected concerns of humanity.

The problems of humanity, of other species and the entire planet have crushingly become ours.

For survival, we must greet this bewildering array of issues in the outer world by grace from within, *by our own honoring of our design*.

Our children can begin to experience fulfillment as soon as we choose to create environments permitting them to do so.

MIND AS
AN OPEN SYSTEM

PART II

A First Look at Open Systems and Children

Looking at the world as a pattern of systems is popular with many professionals. They are creating theories, developing technologies and making much about the utility of the "systems" perspectives in helping us understand how things work. Although much of their work is beyond the focus of this book, a little is helpful here.

OPENMIND/WHOLEMIND is concerned with differences between open and closed systems. Buckminster Fuller described it this way to me: "If you draw a circle in the sand and study only what's inside the circle, then that is a closed-system perspective. If you study what is inside the circle *and* everything outside the circle, then *that* is an open-system perspective."

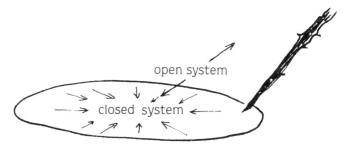

Bucky and many others have eloquently criticized past efforts to treat, for the sake of convenience, open systems as though they were closed. Physicists have done this in formulating the laws of thermodynamics. Psychologists have followed with mechanistic theories of behavior. Educators have institutionalized the three Rs and standardized testing. Contemporary science is encouraging an entirely new era of exploration, not because there are massive new discoveries, but rather because scientists are looking at old knowledge in new ways. They have begun to look at the information outside our equations as well as that contained within.

Education and parenting are also part of this transformation of perspective. What formerly was relevant in our teaching and parenting practices must be re-examined in the light of a new ecology of communication and information.

No longer are children confined to the McGuffey readers and rules of the 1800s household. They have free access to the world outside the limiting circles drawn for them by history. They are edging outward to explore the open systems of reality. Television's situation comedies are challenging them with moral issues that in an earlier era they wouldn't face until adulthood. As parents and teachers, we must choose whether to attempt to stuff them back into the "safety" of yesterday's circles or to facilitate their passage into a world they can co-create.

The themes of encouraging, enhancing and honoring open-system experiences for children make up the major fabric of this book. What are some of the basic assumptions underlying open-system experiences? First, there are no wholly open-system experiences in our day-to-day lives. Systematic knowledge, folkways, mores and customs are always present. And, as stressed earlier, language provides our most intimate experience with closedness. The specific meanings of words and the limits of vocabulary restrict us to saying what is agreed upon rather than what we really experience. Anyone who has tried to describe a "paranormal" experience knows what this means. The philosophy of behaviorism essentially argues that there *is* no openness in human affairs. Behaviorists contend that we are confined to the prisons of our past experience. In my view, this behaviorally-imposed closedness is more a matter of choice than of conditioning.

Now as never before we need the imagination, the dedication, the creativity of everyone to get society through the massive transformation required for a planetary society.
Margaret Mead

What constitutes closedness? Recall the example used earlier about knowing the "right" answer. Certainty about the correctness of a single answer represents closedness. When children are told that "HOT" is bad or dangerous, they are taught that in an absolute way. They eventually will have to unlearn the unequivocal badness of "HOT" to enjoy steamy cocoa or simmering soup. Similarly, because they are told that some things fall "down" and some fly "up," they will eventually be confused by concepts of relativity. Much of what children experience in the name of learning must later be undone. Buckminster Fuller claimed that far more than half of his education was better described as "indoctrination in misinformation." Fuller dedicated his career to correcting the closed-system misinformation he was taught in school.

What I am calling open-system education and parenting is certainly not totally free of misinformation, nor is it devoid of warnings about something that is "HOT." The difference is that all information is presented in such a way that options are kept open. "HOT," for instance, can be presented as an invitation to explore an idea. Our own child was introduced to "HOT" via a lit candle. Candle flames are hot enough to burn but generally not hot enough to maim. With the candle flame, the concept "HOT" can be imbedded in a context that includes the beauty of the flame, the meals served in its light, the composition of the candle, as well as the pain of a burned finger.

Thus the open-system parent or teacher explores concepts freely but respectfully. Closed-system approaches provide *the* specific answer while open system-approaches extend the possibilities.

At the end of a closed-system experience, the learner will have exactitude but little else. Anyone who has taught elementary school knows the feeling that accompanies the announcement of the next unit of study. *"Magnets,"* the teacher proclaims, "will be the next unit we will study in science." The students groan and complain, "We studied that last year." Obviously, they have had a closed-system experience with magnets.

Open-system experience is contextual. That means each experience is related to a host of different conditions. In open-system experiences children do not learn facts—they learn relationships. For example, if "magnets" were presented in an open-system way, children would freely explore the possibilities of magnetism as well as the basic facts. Their minds would reach far beyond simple descriptions of a magnet's differing polarities. They would be ready to imagine the trek of Marco Polo and the magic iron needle carried in a wagon across Asia. They would be ready for further exploration of Northern and Southern lights. They would watch organisms under a microscope snap into alignment when a magnetic field was induced.

We cannot fault teachers and parents for perpetuating closedness without first looking into society's mirror and observing the myriad attractions that have drawn us away from openness. Let us leave the child's mind for a moment and explore our own. How have past and present sculpting by the world affected us?

The Paradox of Brain-Mind Design

Each human being is an open system. The human mind is the ultimate open system. Just when it begins working is a fascinating question. Does a child begin to think at the moment of birth or when those powerful uterine contractions begin to propel him or her through the birth canal? Many researchers have detected brain wave activity far earlier than birth. Rapid eye movement (REM) which accompanies dreaming and brain waves typical of the dream state can be detected months before birth. This suggests an even more intriguing question—if a child dreams in utero, what is he or she dreaming about?

Erich Jantsch, a systems theorist, postulated two major forms of human consciousness: *virtual* and *reflective*. *Virtual consciousness* is the innate form which governs relationships in sub-atomic particles, atoms, molecules and in more complex natural elements. Virtual consciousness provides the "guidance" for water (H_2O) to be constructed exactly the same way whether it comes from a Colorado lake, a Tibetan glacier or Mars.

Virtual consciousness is a built-in context which engages the human mind with the patterns of all creation. It is virtual consciousness that likely guides a child's dreaming in utero. Perhaps it is a biologically-established way for the brain-mind to "practice" before experiencing the world outside the mother. The human mind may well be an expression of virtual consciousness—a template, as it were, imposed on us by an immense voyage through eons of time, that prepares us to act upon the universe.

One can say that *virtual* consciousness is the action the universe takes on us while *reflective* consciousness is the action we take upon the universe. *Reflective consciousness* is *intentional* thought. It acts within the constraints of our biological design but turns out to be boundless. We can reflect upon experience and make decisions about whether or not to repeat that experience. Moreover, we can, through reflection, think about experiences we never had. Jean Piaget called this formal operational thought; it permits us to play games with thought. We can create scenarios wholly within our minds: fight battles, risk resources or even design better worlds. This process is called thinking and the rules by which we play the game are called reasoning.

This brings us full circle back to the issue of open- and closed- systems. Our brain-mind design consisting of *virtual* and *reflective* consciousness has prepared us to be open-system thinkers. Not only are we meant to play the games of mind but *we are designed to write the rules as well*. Paradoxically, the effect of rules is to create closed systems.

Once the closed system of rules enters consciousness, thought begins to serve the rules. The brain-mind seems to give up its creative and formative functions and shifts to maintenance. In other words, reflective consciousness willfully turns itself into a form of self-imposed virtual consciousness. The mind imprisons itself in closedness and this self-imprisonment is buttressed by "reason" and closed-system rationale. The human mind has been taught to give itself the excuse to deny its very design, accepting closedness and permanent limits.

Fuller once likened closedness to selfishness and openness to generosity. He said, "The generous and compassionate propensity of humans is primarily syntropic. The selfish are entropic." Syntropic is derived from the word synergy. Synergy is what open systems do. Closedness is merely a temporary convenience in synergic systems; the dominant process is one of continuous change and adaptation. Synergy is energy-producing. Entropy is energy-consuming. Entropy is the degree of disorder and decay in closed systems. Selfishness is entropic—and so is the selfish mind.

For the selfish mind, knowledge is a commodity to be acquired, hoarded and withheld. The human energy that is required to do this results in eventual decay and disorder—entropy. Selfishness is characterized by relationships that require high maintenance.

There is luck in everything. My luck is that I was born cross-eyed.
R. Buckminster Fuller

Generosity is synergic. The generous mind considers knowledge as a commodity, subject to continuous engagement and change. The exchange of knowledge produces greater numbers of options and continued ability to establish a dynamic order—synergy. Generosity is characterized by relationships that evolve and require little maintenance.

Both closed-system selfishness and open-system generosity are options in the design of the brain-mind system.

The human mind is discovering ways to reverse its habitual closedness and reacknowledge its evolutionary tendencies toward openness. After the mind surveys the basic attributes of the body and brain, it extends and amplifies them. Humans learned to extend musculature by amplifying it with levers, pulleys and gears. Later on humans invented the wheel, the wing and the rocket. Eventually the rocket became the engine and we struck out for other worlds. Our species also extended and amplified the senses. The telescope introduced us to the galaxies and the microscope led us to the microcosm of structures that make up the universe. Microphones, telephones, audio probes, sonar extended hearing, and now the worlds of computers, information processing and artificial intelligence extend our capacities to reason. The mind, that ultimate of open systems, is now pushing back its own limits at a pace that can hardly be sensed.

Yet we live in a world constructed of our history—and history has not been kind to our design. The cultural tendencies toward selfishness have created boundary lines on maps, national flags and bureaucracies brimming with rules and regulations of conduct. Schools, churches and courts of law have created overlapping versions of closed-system experience. Competition is seen as an ethic and lays the foundation of personal and public selfishness. Selfishness and the closed systems it spawns have provided the warp and woof of historical consciousness. Our mind's reductive heritage is a cloak that threatens to suffocate our design.

The true pioneering effort of modern times is to re-learn how to honor open systems. It is an effort that is being suppressed by centuries of habit.

We have entered a new paradigm of thought. A paradigm is a pattern, an example, a model. When we enter a new paradigm, little that came before is sustained by it. In his fascinating book, *The Promise Of The Coming Dark Age*, Leften Stavrianos demonstrates that major shifts in basic patterns of thinking took place not during the Renaissance but during the Dark Ages. The Renaissance resulted from the transformation of thought that occurred during the Dark Ages.

Contemporary authors of widely-divergent expertise arrive at similar conclusions about the present age. We live in an age of transformation. Marilyn Ferguson's *Aquarian Conspiracy* was the first synthesis; Fritjof Capra, a physicist, and Rupert Sheldrake, a plant physiologist, followed with their own, suggesting that the movement toward openness and toward open-system approaches is real and underway. A veritable choir is heralding the arrival of open-system thought and approaches.

The significance of all this to parenting and teaching is that our current perspective of how the mind works differs greatly from that of the past. As noted earlier, we once felt that the brain was like a mental file cabinet where order and structure prevail. We determined it would best be served by orderly and structured experiences. Parenting and schooling were designed to provide specific closed-system training. Routine and discipline were seen as virtues rather than conveniences. Children came to be judged by how well they conformed to closed-system rules. They quickly learned to play the game to *win*. It was seldom their prerogative to learn how to write new rules and thus open up their own systems of thought. Pitiably, growing up meant fitting in—conforming to the rules which, once written, were seldom questioned.

As stated earlier, with television, visual and auditory media and computer access today's children can simply by-pass such attempts to limit their experience. The so called "shallow" TV situation comedies and even the Saturday morning cartoons address issues that are years away from textbook or standard school curriculum coverage. Racism, sexism and other bigotries are exposed through entertainment. The values and customs of contemporary life are held up to question each evening. News broadcasts usher into the child's consciousness clandestine war, apartheid, injustice and hypocrisy.

As parents, we are being asked far more difficult questions than ever before. Fathers and mothers are yearning for "the old days" when the most-feared responsibility of parenting was to disclose the "facts of life." Now the questions center around unwanted pregnancy, homosexuality, AIDS and herpes. Divorce affects every family—either directly or indirectly through friends. But, at the same time, questions emerge about world hunger, the arms race and global peace. The lyrics of popular music contain topics central to the lives of the twenty-first-century child—drugs, relationships and thermonuclear war. Try as we may, we cannot enforce a closed-system life for our children. We cannot go "back to the basics" and the fantasy of the values expressed in 1950s films. Today, in our homes, schools, churches and workplaces, we are required to instill an ethic evolving from open-system possibility, not closed-system repression.

What, then, is our choice? I suggest it is as simple as honoring the reality of experience in our world. It requires that we stop relying on the comfortable myths of history. It requires that we accede to what is known about the design of the brain-mind system, repelling rigidity and nurturing mental flexibility. This may involve possibly painful re-examinations of our own attitudes and beliefs about learning, decision-making, living. Our egos may suffer as we falter and stumble through this deliberate renaissance. But the rewards are worth the effort, for we will acquire for our children and ourselves the skills of survival. All the tomorrows are tentative. We need courage to greet the tentative.

The closed mind is the mind of the bigot . . . it is a mind imprisoned within a region of all-pervasive and unquestioned "truth."

Expressions of Open-System Thought

As a teacher or parent, my first and most important preparation is to determine whether or not I am closed about what I choose to offer a child. *I must ask myself if in my own mind what I choose to share is closed or open.* If an idea is closed, I must take care to offer it in an open way.

Let's explore this with a specific example. I confess that in the past I have been fairly closed about acts of violence between children. I tended to react in kind; that is, I grabbed the warring parties by their arms, shook them and told them in no uncertain terms what I thought about their behavior. It was years before I was able to understand that children fight because they see no other options. Violence reflects an optionless perspective. My violent response simply reinforced this position. It doesn't make much sense to hit a child in order to teach him or her that hitting is a bankrupt solution. Let me describe my first departure from this posture.

I was confronted on a playground by two children who were fighting, Ted and Jimmie. Ted was bleeding from his lip and sobbing in humiliation and pain. Jimmie, with an injured hand, was also crying but his tears resulted from frustration and perhaps fear. He was trying vainly to hold Ted's arms down against his sides, to calm him and prevent him from retaliating. I told them both to stop, but was ignored. As soon as Jimmie let go, Ted started swinging wildly. I slipped forward and held Ted in a firm but gentle hug. Jimmie, obviously relieved, said desperately, "I didn't mean to hit you . . . it was an accident." He repeated it several times.

Ted would have none of it. He shouted back, "It was no accident and I'm going to bust you right back." I asked Ted if he really intended to hit Jimmie. He said yes. I had a real closed-system stand-off on my hands.

I asked Ted where he planned to hit Jimmie. "Right in the mouth, just like he hit me."

"Oh come now, that's too easy. Besides, you'll hurt your hand like he did," I said. Then I asked Jimmie to hold up his hand. It was bleeding from an open cut.

"What else could you do?" I asked.

"I could hit him in the gut," he said with less anger in his voice.

"What could you do other than hitting him?" I could feel his body begin to relax.

"I could tear his shirt," said now-released Ted.

"Interesting." I replied. "What else?"

"I could tear up his arithmetic homework," said Ted with a wisp of a smile crossing his swollen lip.

"That is a really wicked thing to do." I turned to Jimmie and asked, "What do you think he could do to get even?"

Jimmie said, "He could steal the cookie out of my lunch."

"I could spit in your milk at break time," Ted offered, now smiling fully.

"Bending pencils 'til the lead breaks is a real dirty trick." said Jimmie.

Both were smiling now and Ted saw the blood on my shirt and apologized. I asked them if they knew how to get blood stains out of clothes. Neither did, so I told them about how hot water fixes blood in clothes and that cold water is best. As we walked back to the school building, both of them were laughing uproariously at the dirty tricks they had thought up. As they disappeared into the school building I heard Jimmie say, *"Spit in my milk . . . Yuk!"* It was clear that I was no longer needed except to tell their homeroom teacher that they might need a bit of tending to.

All I did was increase their options. The code of the playground was clear: If someone hits you, you hit back. There are no other options in such a setting. Often teachers and parents muddle the issue by going for "justice." They ask whose fault it was, who hit first, why were they fighting. These attempts simply focus the children's attention on the legitimacy of the code. Hitting back is the "right" answer in that closed system. By asking for alternative kinds of "revenge" I created the possibility that the code henceforth might be more flexible. I also increased the likelihood that both boys might learn to see the humor in events before resorting to violence.

In a way, this example is the heart of this book. *We can parent and teach in ways that increase childrens' options.* In pages to come we will explore in detail the openness of the brain-mind system. Closed minds are closed by choice and habit rather than design. When I hear a child say, "We studied magnets last year," I am reminded of the child who says, "You hit me so I'll hit you back." These are the reactions of children well on their way to forming closed minds. These are children who have already had too many years of closed-system approaches. Such children view new experiences as work rather than as mind's play and adventure.

Parents and teachers often teach closed-mindedness by approaching skills, facts and values in closed-system ways. For example, I saw a teacher teaching the relationship "2+2" as a closed system. For her the answer was always "4." It could be written either of the following ways:

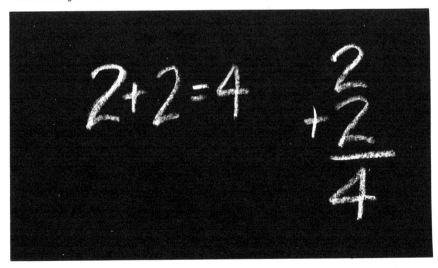

But in either case the answer was the same. I teased her about her closedness and at first her only response was a blank stare. It was, after all, the right answer, she argued. I agreed that it was, but only in a narrow sense. It was true arithmetically but not true metaphorically. She pointed out that she was teaching arithmetic, not metaphor. I reminded her that people who think metaphorically always have more options than do those who only stress the accuracy and precision of closed-system facts. I also reminded her about studies showing that a majority of adults hated math. For most, math is perceived as drudgery. Actually, the studies demonstrated that these adults didn't hate math as much as they hated what they experienced when they took math in school.

The next day the teacher allowed me to teach during arithmetic hour. I went to the board and wrote 2+2=3. At first there was a good deal of giggling and teasing. I was told I was wrong and the real answer was "4." After that there was silence. I told the children that the answer "3" was the only answer I had that day and they had to help me show that it was a right answer. Seconds ticked by and silence dragged on. Finally a little girl with a mischievous smile said that "the right answer was 3 because the equal sign was a bridge. Under that bridge lived a troll. Every time numbers tried to cross the bridge, the troll ate one of the numbers as it passed over."

The class erupted in giggles which quickly subsided as they waited to see what I would say. "That's a great answer," I said and asked for other explanations. Staying close to the original answer, the next child claimed that the equal sign was a bridge, but in this instance a toll bridge and the keeper charged a fee of "1" to let the other three pass over.

Another said that a 4 is three ones. I had trouble with that until the child went to the board and wrote the following:

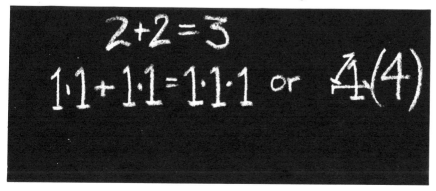

The teacher was delighted, as were the children. The experience took the absoluteness out of numerical expression. In addition, it gave the children the opportunity to demonstrate flexibility and playfulness in their thinking. This teacher and dozens of others in subsequent years reported that when they used these playful approaches, enthusiasm for arithmetic increased remarkably. They also reported higher skills acquisition and greater understanding of mathematical concepts.

There are certainly those who claim that such approaches nurture a soft-headedness and that children will never grow up knowing right from wrong. More often than not, such criticism is based on the dread that there will be a loss of control. *Control is the primary concern of closed-system thinkers.* The most closed of the psychological theories, behaviorism, is totally committed to control.

A Glance at Behaviorism

We have so recently emerged from the dominating influence of behaviorism on our educational institutions that open-system approaches are rarely understood. Behaviorism was popular in schools because behavioral goals and objectives could be stated at the beginning of the year and measured at the end. Somehow, this appealed to educators who held an assembly-line vision of the educational process. For such educators, school was a place to "assemble" the minds and bodies of students according to established blueprints.

Educational technologies based on behaviorism continue to attract followers. A program called ITIP (Improving Teaching and Instructional Performance) authored by Madeline Hunter is foremost among these. The primary mission of ITIP is to develop specific teacher behaviors that reward favorable student responses and performances in the basic skills of reading, writing, and arithmetic. Strangely, it also has been used to "reward" behaviors that insure control. The popularity of the program is based less on the fact that it improves student performance than that it provides external criteria for evaluating teachers. Astute teachers quickly have perceived that the program benefits the administration more than the students.

The proponents of behaviorism fail to see that their results are basically trivial and that their approaches simply do not challenge the awesome design of the brain-mind system. Behaviorism as a philosophy embodies identifiable closedness. It requires *an* answer to each situation. In the earlier example of the playground fight, I did not predetermine a course of action. Instead, I rid myself of pre-conceptions and followed options that emerged.

If they saw it as useful, behaviorists would attempt to turn my response into a technique. It would be packaged in a "shrink-wrap" of efficiency and marketed as *the* answer to playground conflict. Specific criteria would be established and external evaluation made possible.

The problem then is to understand how something that begins so well can often end so badly. Margaret Donaldson

41

Forming habits is raised to an art form by schooling. Unfortunately they are mostly habits that repress the mind.

The bankruptcy of behaviorism is that it is anti-evolutionary. Its fundamental outcome is the preservation of a narrow and specialized kind of conformity and sameness. It designates the parent or teacher as the administrator of a technique rather than a dynamic player in an open-ended process of evolution within the brain-mind system. In natural systems, limited options and specialization result in homogeneity. Homogeneity leads to extinction. Diversity nurtures evolutionary continuity.

I often like to tell a story about the "liberation" of a half-dozen pigeons from a behavior modification laboratory. Behaviorists love to study pigeons, perhaps because the pigeons choose cooperation over boredom when studied. The pigeons in question had been trained to walk in circles both clockwise and counterclockwise. They had also been taught to slap ping-pong balls with the side of their beaks so as to gain food.

All the birds in this story were adept in these tasks. They performed daily for their food and thus confirmed the efficiency of the researchers' training. Now about their liberation. One evening, a group of somewhat intoxicated conspirators decided to take the pigeons from the lab and return them to a natural setting. Arguments raged about what the birds would do: Would they continue with the behaviors they learned in the labs? Would they revert to normal pigeon behavior or flutter around, confused and helpless?

Eventually the time came to find out which view was correct. The pigeons were taken from the lab and carried to a public park. Once out of the cages, the pigeons began to act precisely like the other pigeons there. They flew, they cooed, they pecked and at no time circled clockwise or counterclockwise. Once in the open system of the natural world, these highly-conditioned birds reverted to exercising the basic skills of evolutionary continuity.

On a hot summer night in a stifling auditorium in Marin County, California, Gregory Bateson and Carl Rogers debated, among other things, the nature of behaviorism. On this evening, several years before his death, Bateson admonished Rogers, a senior scholar in humanistic psychology, about his adamant anti-behaviorism stance. He warned that "new age" psychologies were unrealistically pretending that behaviorism didn't exist. Bateson argued that we should recognize behaviorism for the trivial form of coercion training that it is and get on with creating psychologies that stretch toward the grander design of the brain-mind system.

OPENMIND/WHOLEMIND attempts to do precisely that. Closed-system thought is a real option, but it is one that always requires reinforcement. If our children are trained and educated in behaviorism, we as parents and teachers must willingly turn them over to closed societies that will reward them for pigeon-like twirling and batting of ping-pong balls in someone else's game. Closed minds can only enforce what *was*. What *could be* is the dominion of openness.

A primary claim of those who defend closed systems is that they are efficient. *Efficiency* means "doing the job well." But educators have been growing concerned about whether this is enough. For many, the concept of effectiveness must be considered. *Effectiveness* is more than "doing the job well;" it is doing *the most appropriate* job well. In closed and "efficient" systems, the "right" answer is the most sought. In open systems, "rightness" depends upon how thoroughly the learner has honored the things *outside* Buckminster Fuller's circle. Efficiency is always gauged *inside* the circle; effectiveness requires attention both inside and out. The pigeons were efficient in the laboratory but became effective again only when they were allowed *outside* the "circle."

Structure and closedness are not absent from open systems, but they are always temporary and open to expansion and change. In closed systems, structure and closedness are mandated for purposes of control. The concepts of right and wrong exist in both systems. In open systems, right and wrong are emergent qualities which envelop and define grace, or "fit." In closed systems, they are predetermined and fixed, causing an inordinate amount of energy to be spent trying to avoid or deny the inevitable: change.

Habits of Thought

Abraham Maslow once said that if I think of myself as a hammer I will treat the rest of the world like a nail. I am continually amazed when I rediscover how powerfully belief affects perception. Many have heard stories about how well supposedly below-average students perform when placed in classes for the gifted. Others note that remarkable feats are accomplished when people are simply told they *can* do something. I remember an acquaintance who once became violently ill on spoiled canned milk. Convinced it would make him sick, he avoided canned milk for the rest of his life. His response was classically behavioral: He created self-imposed closedness toward experience based on one dramatic stimulus.

Some people refuse to let experience interfere with habit. When North Americans hear the word "breakfast" they think of eggs, bacon, toast, milk or coffee, or, perhaps cereal and fruit. Hardly any conjure up images of Fettucini Alfredo, anchovy salad and Soave Blanc.

The same kinds of habits limit our thinking about the human brain and its most exciting creation—the human mind. Our perceptions of the brain-mind system derive from our accumulated heritage as citizens of a technocratic culture.

As Western science developed, it became deeply committed to creating understanding by taking things apart, including the brain. Yet other cultures had studied the functions of the mind for centuries and had not cut brains out of bodies. Such studies were viewed by Western scientists as second rate because they didn't link effects with causes. To understand any action it was necessary to find out what caused it. Since the brain was supposed to be the origin of thought, the brain, not thought, had to be studied.

Our dictionaries reflect the Western model. Consider the following definition of the brain:

> The mass of nerve tissue in the cranium of vertebrate animals, an enlarged extension of the spinal cord. [2]

The mind is defined as follows:

> The element, part, substance or process that reasons, thinks, feels, wills, perceives, judges, etc; the processes of the mind; the totality of conscious and unconscious mental processes and activities of the organism. [3]

There seems to be more "science" in the definition of brain than in the definition of mind. Descriptions of an organ that can be measured, weighed and sliced apart provide the "facts" science demands. Even now, the brain is the object of intensive study and earlier ideas about its functioning are being modified almost daily. New technologies used in brain study are actually restoring the mystery to our understanding of the brain in the same way the cyclotron restored mystery to the study of the atom.

Mind is more unknown and unmeasurable. Philosophers as well as physicians and psychologists have vainly tried to establish agreement about what the mind is and how it works. Perhaps we are no closer now than were the authors of the Sumerian creation epics, thousands of years B.C. They worried that their hero, Gilgamesh, had two minds in his brain, "neither of which was to be understood."

Ironically, when we consider the work of the mind, we consider the more exact, measurable and precise as the most favorable. In our culture, reason and rationality have the highest respect and authority. In other cultures reason and rationality are not as prized as mystical insight and shamanistic vision. Both world views have survived and flourished for tens of thousands of years.

The bias toward reason and rationality is central to the Western vision of preferred brain function. In accord with this bias, people with "good" brains think rationally and understand reason. They often become doctors, lawyers, engineers and scientists. They are considered to be the ones who set the standards for how brains should work.

Other people, who seem to know a lot but who can't express themselves in terms of reason and rationality, are considered to have inferior brains. They are called poets, artists, dancers and athletes. Their gifts are capriciousness and unpredictability. Their ideas and contributions often do not fit into the frameworks established by reason and rationality.

Artists are really much nearer to the truth than many of the scientists.
R. Buckminster Fuller

Freud and the Unconscious

Sigmund Freud was one of the first modern theorists to address this issue of differences in patterns of thought. His studies of the mind distinguished between rational and irrational thought. Rational thought conforms to what the culture "understands," or considers logical and reasonable. Irrational thought distorts and refuses to conform to established rationality.

To house these warring elements of mind function, Freud invented two domains of consciousness, the Rational Conscious Domain and the Irrational Unconscious Domain. Freud held that a person's commitment to and utilization of rational conscious processes constituted mental health. When one became victimized by the unconscious domain, one became vulnerable to mental illness. This relationship is illustrated in the diagram below:

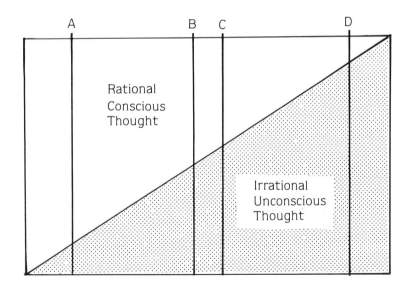

FIGURE I

The light part of this figure represents a person's preference for rational thought as the mode of processing experience. The shaded field represents one's reliance on the irrational unconscious realm as the dominant mode of thought processing. Freud would say Person A was mentally healthy since the person spends most of his or her time in the rational consciousness mode. Only a small amount of processing time is dominated by unconscious thought.

Persons B and C are borderline or unreliable people in Freud's model, as they spend about half of their processing time in each domain. Person D is in serious trouble. Nearly 90% of this subject's thought style is in the realm of the unconscious. Freud viewed Person D as extremely neurotic or psychotic and a probable candidate for institutionalization.

Freud was influenced by the scientific world view of his time—a world view dominated by the earlier philosophical traditions of Descartes and Isaac Newton. Both of these thinkers were enamored with logic and rational thought. In addition, both had powerful allegiances to cause-and-effect relationships. Clearly, Freud was a Newtonian pioneer in the theories of mind.

Freud's work has had a lasting impact. Freud saw the unconscious as a seething cauldron of unspoken wishes, fantasies and repressed aggression. It is a world that logic and rationality could not penetrate. It is the womb of mental illness.

Perhaps the most damaging of Freud's conclusions about the mind has to do with creativity. Creative people, claimed Freud, are irrational victims of unconscious dominance. Creative people challenge the patterns of rational convention by trying to change things. They toss aside logic and rationality and invent things that cannot be easily understood. Such activity is clearly irrational according to Freud's model.

Kubie's Challenge: Creativity and the Preconscious

An avid researcher and follower of Freud later challenged this point of view. His name was Lawrence Kubie. Kubie argued that creative people are not more neurotic and psychotic than others. He maintained that creative people rely on a different domain of thinking not at all as debilitating as the unconscious processes. This new, third realm Kubie termed the *Preconscious*. Kubie inserted the Preconscious realm between the Rational Conscious and the Irrational Unconscious domains, as shown in Figure II.

Figure II

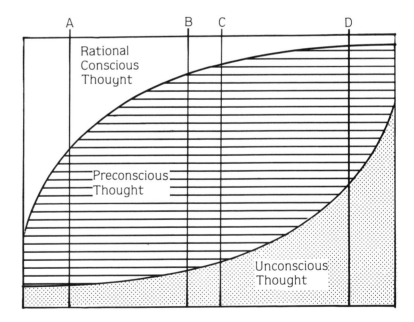

Kubie argued that preconscious thought makes people creative and that too much unconscious thought actually distorts creativity as surely as it distorts rational thought.

Typical examples of preconscious thought include night dreaming, day dreaming (self-induced imagery), guided imagery, fantasy, visualization, meditation, repetitive movement, reveries, auditory and olfactory recall and dozens of other experiences. Very likely, *deja vu*, prescience, precognition, telepathy, telekinesis and dream transmission also are related to preconscious processes.

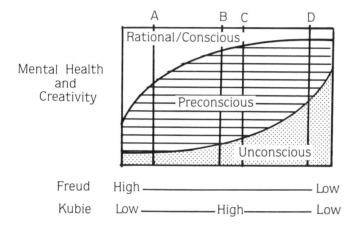

Figure III

Many of Kubie's conclusions rest on his research with low-level hypnosis. Kubie found that people subjected to mild hypnotic suggestions are far better able to remember and list out-of-sight items than those who do not receive the suggestions.

After much exploration, Kubie concluded that the rational mind remembers what it understands, while the preconscious remembers what it doesn't understand. None of this, by the way, negates Freud's concept of unconscious processes. Rather, Kubie simply extended Freud's work by adding a zone on each side of his original boundary. It is this accessible preconscious zone that children so readily explore and that adults seem to lose as they grow up. I am convinced, like Kubie, that creativity is an indicator of high mental health. Many contemporary psychologists and therapists are also convinced that rational neurosis, a compulsion or overcommitment to rational thought and understanding, may well be the dominant form of mental illness in our society today.

My work in creativity has convinced me that creative people are those who have retained the capability from childhood to accept what they understand and also what they do not understand. Moreover they seem to enjoy access to both. They are not disrespectful of conventional knowledge but neither do they stand in awe of it.

The adult creative are never sure if they have retained from childhood their acceptance of the unknown, or if they have relearned it. I don't think it matters. I have come to believe that anyone can reinstate access to the preconscious or simply establish a new path.

I have tried in my work to preserve the child's honoring of preconscious access and to encourage adults to re-access. Creative people are exciting; their resourcefulness inspires day-to-day living. They relate to others openly and loyally, experience fewer stress-induced diseases and greet unexpected changes, whether pleasant or disastrous, with a sense of adventure.

To recapture childhood's wonder is to secure a driving force for grown-up thoughts.
Charles Sherrington

Models of the mind thus can confine or liberate us. As Maslow said about the hammer and nail, we are travelers on the paths laid by our metaphors. Freud was enamored of dyadic metaphors and those of gears, machines, levers and pulleys. Kubie added a single dimension to that mechanistic model and transformed it into one far more open. He reinstated the virtue of the unknown in mind function—bringing the human being back into the role of sculpting experience.

Fortunately, the brain was not to remain on the bottom of the dissecting tray. It has risen to five decades of scientific research that have restored its mystery.

Those who study the brain have been divested of a Newtonian certainty which served to shield them from the unknown. Humility and awe now guide explorations of the brain-mind system.

HOLONOMY: AN OPEN MODEL FOR THE OPEN MIND

PART III

Models of the Brain-Mind System

The brain-mind system has been studied for centuries. Far from being closer to a complete understanding of its forms and functions, we stand sometimes bewildered but always fascinated by its galactic complexity. Mystical beauty and ordered reason guide our journey.

The vision of the universe as a great machine was held dear by Copernican and Newtonian astronomers and physicists in the 1800s and early 1900s. When early neuroscientists began to explore brain function through surgery, they quickly fell victim to their metaphors. As they stimulated the brain with electrical impulses and caused reactions in different parts of the body, they began to think of the brain and nervous system as wiring and circuitry. "Throwing the switches" and "turning on the lights" became common expressions for memory. "Getting the gears turning" and "putting things on the back burner" are still widely used.

Today, the computer is the most popular metaphor for brain-mind function. Again the metaphor is impoverished. No single computer nor any combination of computers can emulate even the most trivial of brain-mind processes. The brain possesses a universe of functions, all of which contribute to a network of redundancy and replication that baffles understanding. Nobel prizes have been won for the determination of remarkably simple things about the brain. Even with the significant research that is being conducted we stand as children before a mysterious domain that we are unlikely to ever fully understand.

But with all that, we still are able to use our brains and minds to explore and create meaning in the world. One of the most baffling questions we face is how the brain can study itself. How can this be? How can billions of nerve cells, tossed together in massive neuroelectrical and magnetic storms, bathed in an ocean of detailed molecules, facilitate the forces of memory, problem solving and creativity? How can we even think about thinking?

Two of the more popular contemporary models of brain-mind function help us see that, if asked properly, the mind can do remarkable things. These models are the lateralized brain and the triune brain. The first emphasizes functions, right and left. The second explores functions from bottom to top.

The Lateralized Brain

On Christmas Eve a few years ago, my mother suffered an intense but localized stroke. A bursting blood vessel in her brain allowed a quantity of blood to seep into the brain tissue causing a build-up of pressure and eventually a clot. The clot and the pressure it created destroyed a portion of my mother's brain. When brain tissue is destroyed, a loss of function occurs somewhere in the body.

My mother's stroke caused mild paralysis on her right side and a near-total loss of speech, reading and writing ability. However, she was able to comprehend what she heard, hum tunes, and draw and paint images that were accurate as well as graceful.

Thousands of other stroke cases have yielded similar results. Such damage is overwhelmingly traced to injury to the left cerebral hemisphere. In the upper part or cerebrum of the brain are two large lobes or hemispheres. Stroke or accident damage to one or the other of these hemispheres results in the loss of different functions. Left-hemisphere damage nearly always affects speech and various language functions, whereas right-hemisphere damage hardly ever does. Through history, the left hemisphere has come to be called the major hemisphere and the right the minor hemisphere. This terminology shows the power of our priority on language and the logic of expression.

During the last two decades, neurophysiologists have explored this brain lateralization. Noted researchers such as Joseph Bogen, Michael Gazzaniga, David Galin and Robert Ornstein have led the exploration. Most luminous, perhaps, is Roger Sperry, who won the Nobel Prize in 1981 for his work.

These researchers and others provided convincing evidence that the two hemispheres of the brain do in fact possess a division of labor, as it were. They found that the left cortex specializes in rational, logical, linear, sequential and time-ordered processing. Since language is wedded to all these descriptors, a left-hemisphere stroke, such as my mother's, affects these functions. The right hemisphere in most people specializes in analogic, metaphoric, holistic, visual-spatial and synthesizing functions. Because of this specialization, my mother retained the ability to draw, paint and hum music, all of which tend to be right-hemisphere functions. Figure IV summarizes brain lateralization.

Left Hemisphere   Right Hemisphere

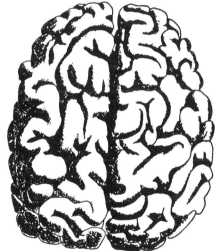

Figure IV

RATIONAL   METAPHORIC
LOGICAL   ANALOGIC
LINEAR   HOLISTIC
SEQUENTIAL   VISUAL-SPATIAL
TIME-ORDERED   SYNTHETIC

Research demonstrates that the two hemispheres function in a complementary way. Unfortunately, this research supports those who like to see things in black and white. It has provided false substance for a new dichotomy—one separating "left-brained" and "right-brained" persons. There is substance to the claim that people develop mental habits as surely as they develop physical ones. Hemispheric dominance is expressed in a variety of ways, particularly in styles of learning, problem resolution and often lifestyle. But a person can never abandon the influence of one or the other hemisphere.

In teaching and parenting, we are biased toward the qualities of left-hemisphere processing. More than one neuroscientist has described schools as "half-brained" institutions. And in homes, how often are the displaced egos of frustrated parents used as funnels of narrowness to force children into achievement in the left hemisphere skills? If students are narrow in ways school approve of, they are most often called gifted. Sometimes parents try to force this narrowness in child rearing so that success in school will be insured. Occasionally after I have delivered a speech on the topic of left and right hemisphere specialization, agitated parents will rush to the podium and demand to know where they can find a "right-brained" school for their child. Such parents, who feel victimized by the schools' over-emphasis on left-brain approaches, appear ready to sentence their children to the mirror image of such narrowness. Separation in parenting or schooling is not the solution. Holism is. *When schools honor the whole brain, all children will benefit.*

We know more than we
can tell.
Michael Polanyi

The Triune Brain: A Vertical Model

The neuroscientists who study brain function from an evolutionary standpoint are convinced of another way of separating brain function. For these scientists, the human brain is the latest expression of continuous change, and it contains the prior forms that emerged during its evolutionary journey. Dr. Paul MacLean is the most eloquent spokesperson for the three-layered or "triune" brain model.

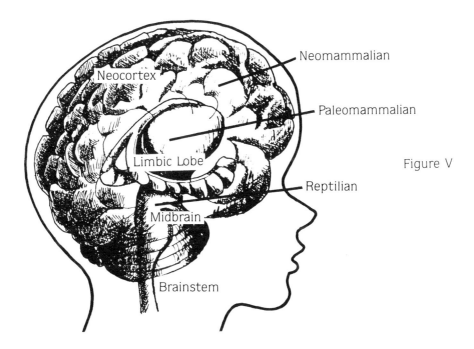

Figure V

The triune brain model is vertical; that is, its definition reflects its structure from bottom to top. The earliest vertebrates began to show brain development with little more than a swelling of neural tissue at the front end of their spinal columns. As time progressed, this minor enlargement began to provide these organisms with a unique survival advantage: the ability to choose to stay where they were or to run or swim away from predators, later called the fight or flight syndrome. Gradually this area enlarged until it represented a brain structure similar to that of contemporary reptiles. (See Figure V.) Experimental research has shown this region of the brain to be linked to hunting, homing, mating, establishing territory and self-preservation. In spite of the derogatory nuance of calling this the "lizard" brain, as many do, it is well to recognize that without these ways of knowing we might not be here. In humans these ways of knowing may be orchestrated into more complex functions—functions that are central to the kinds of fulfillment Maslow spoke of in his philosophy of self-actualization. In the triune model we still possess this brain and it resides in us as the brain stem.

The next noteworthy layer came with an evolutionary blooming of what has come to be called the paleomammalian brain. Within it lies the beautiful and graceful structures of the limbic system. Some say this part of the brain, structurally quite similar to the brain of an arctic fox or a Bengal tiger, provides us with the realm of emotions and has particular memory functions. Again, detractors of the "lower" portions of the brain forget that these functions are as central to the definition of humanness as is reflective thought.

The third layer of the brain in the triune model is the "new" or neomammalian cortex. The descriptions of it are consistent with those in the section on the lateralized brain. The most potentially damaging feature of this triune model is the characterization of their stacked components as hierarchical—from supposedly lower to higher functions. This characterization results in the same form of chauvinism that accompanies all other hierarchical models. The top is best and the bottom is somehow inferior.

We cannot allow such prejudices to shadow the immense grandeur of the design of the human brain. All parts possess integrity. Each part provides synergic contributions to the unity of the whole. Without any part we are less whole and less human. To achieve such a holistic model, scientists have synthesized the lateralized and triune models into the holonomic model. This third model emphasizes metaphors of unity and wholeness.

The Holonomic Brain

My mother's stroke was determined to be local in nature. That is, the damage occupied a specific space in the brain—it was not spread throughout the whole hemisphere. Although localized, the damage was both physical and psychological. Here was a woman who spoke five languages, read incessantly, wrote dozens of letters a month and did crossword puzzles by the hour. Moreover, she had so very much to tell her only grandchild that would enrich both their lives.

I knew my mother would get discouraged and bitter if she felt there was no hope. To avert her despair, I elected to get her to begin drawing and painting as soon as possible. We began at the hospital within forty-eight hours of the stroke. I am not a trained neuroscientist nor am I a stroke recovery therapist. I am, however, a student of the brain-mind system. I studied the work of Dr. Karl Pribram, a neuroscientist at the Stanford University Medical School and one of the most imaginative and charming people I have ever met. From his lectures and publications, I gathered the insight and courage to assist in my mother's recovery.

In my view, Pribram was the first to move beyond the dichotomous trap of lateralized hemisphere research. As a surgeon, Pribram removed portions of damaged and diseased brains. His interest in the patient went far beyond the specific medical recovery. Like many other surgeons, he was also interested in the recovery of the mind.

This interest led him to trace the recovery histories of stroke patients. He noticed that some patients would recover rapidly and in good spirits; others would take three to four times as long to recover and were never in good humor. Nearly all patients with local damage experienced significant if not complete recovery.

Pribram concluded that knowledge is not restricted to a specific part of the brain. He knew that brain tissue had not regenerated in the destroyed areas. He knew there had been no time for re-learning. So he was forced to search elsewhere.

Through a series of events over a span of years, Pribram settled into an exploration of the hologram and holonomy as a primary model for brain-mind organization. A hologram is a medium for recording optical information. In a hologram, all the information is stored in virtually every part of the recording medium. The optical information is stored in frequency patterns rather than as images. The images are retrieved by shining an organizing kind of light (usually laser light) onto the medium. The result is that a three-dimensional frequency image is recreated. With holograms one can see in three-D and can see different perspectives from different angles.

Pribram insightfully compared the way a hologram stores information with the the way the brain stores information. A hologram can be cut into pieces and each piece will contain the information that the original contained. This, perhaps, was how the brain was able to reinstate lost functions so quickly and completely. Pribram concluded that every part of the brain experiences everything the rest of the brain experiences *but it does so it in a different way*. The real task is to create appropriate ways to ask the undamaged brain to express what it knows about a lost function so as to retrieve that function.

Holonomic models are based on wholeness. What this means is that, regardless of how detailed the study of any system is, the parts have to be reassembled into a whole before any real conclusions are reached. For example, when the recovery therapists first treated my mother for loss of speech after her stroke, they isolated her problem to speech. They chose this tiny fragment, of all the things my mother was, to be the "problem" they would address.

On one fateful January day (before we took mother home for her holonomic treatment) the therapist began working on her speech problem. She and mother sat at a table by a window. On the table was a large poinsettia plant, still brilliantly blooming although the holiday season had passed. The therapist carefully and patronizingly explained to mother that they were about to embark on a mission that would help her recover her speech. My mother glanced anxiously at me, belying her lack of enthusiasm for the process that was about to begin.

The therapist reached over and took one of the poinsettia leaves in her hand. She then asked my mother if she could name what she was touching. Mom, resigned to try to oblige, pursed her mouth and slowly said "poy, poy,—" and then shook her head and tried to repeat, "poy, poy, *Poyee*." The therapist smiled encouragingly and said, "That was close, Eve. This is plant . . . *plant*."

Fortunately, she did not see the look my mother shot sideways at me. I knew this therapist was in for a long day. My mother was clearly trying to say *Poinsettia* rather than plant. I shrugged, and mother, plainly miffed, turned back to the therapist. After congratulating mother on getting the "P" sound correct, the therapist next touched a red leaf and asked mother what part of the plant it was. Again, mother pursed her lips and said haltingly, "per, per,—." Then, shaking her head, she said "ped, ped," and sat back in her chair. The therapist told her that that would be all for the day and my mother rose and walked stiffly to her room. The therapist then took me aside and confided that this would be a long, drawn-out process; although mother's first attempt with the "p" sound was encouraging, her next choice of the "p" instead of the "l" sound for "leaf" was not.

I was flabbergasted! The therapist hadn't realized that mother was trying to say "petal," not leaf. She parted and I returned to my mother's room. I found her in a rage. She shook her head and stalked around the room. I laughed at her anger and when she knew that I knew she had done very well in her session, regardless of the therapist's point of view, she began to laugh. She left the hospital and the therapist's care in five days. She came home where her environment was structured to treat her as a whole person with a small handicap, instead of as a speech problem with a useless, helpless person attached. Wholeness is reality—fragmentation is a deviation from that reality.

After the difficult experiences with professional recovery therapists, and my mother had returned to a home setting, we chose not to emphasize speech, reading or writing. Instead we focused on things she loved to do. We asked her to care for the plants and to cook foods for her grandson that she had prepared for me as a child. She would spend hours puttering with the plants and preparing meals. Often she would smell spices and look to the pictures on canned goods. Since she had memorized all the recipes she retrieved them with great ease. In addition to these activities, mother and her grandson practiced word recognition and reading using flashcards.

At first, her progress seemed slow and labored, but gradually the pace picked up remarkably. Occasionally she would say words and often complete sentences with great clarity. These would always be in the proper context. If she was cooking, she commented about cooking. If she was working with plants, she would say something about plants. We never made a show about her accomplishments because we didn't want to draw her attention back to speech and writing. Instead, she wandered freely about her brain for anything that would work for her at the time.

Within three months, she had recovered normal speech and spent hours on the phone talking to relatives and friends. She could read, if the print was large enough, and she could do crossword puzzles slowly but joyfully.

The holonomic or holographic model assumes the brain works in ways that facilitate such a recovery. This model assumes that experience can be recovered in a wide variety of forms and a wide variety of ways. If experience is encoded throughout the brain, information recovery can take place anywhere. We must be ready to recognize how information is retrieved and how to express it in a useful form.

The destruction of a part of the brain seems not to destroy the mind. While it is true that certain functions of the brain may be disturbed, the more holistic qualities of the mind are sustained. The real task is to find ways to inform the recovering person that his or her mind is still active and working in ways other than the ways represented by the lost functions. When this awareness is created, true recovery of the lost functions is greatly facilitated. Much depends on the retrieval strategy. The retrieval strategies or therapeutic foci that resulted in Pribram's differences in patients' recovery rates and attitudes are diagrammed in Figure VI .

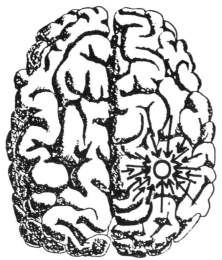

The Pattern of Distribution of
Experience Throughout The Brain
With Therapeutic Focus on Disability

Figure VI.

The Pattern of Distribution of
Experience Throughout The Brain
With Therapeutic Focus on Ability

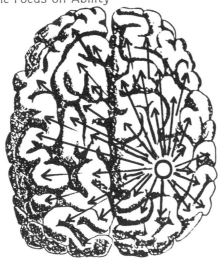

The difference between these should be obvious. When therapy focuses on a disability, the patient's self esteem suffers. The deficit status inhibits the recovery. The patient cannot submit to re-learning—ego gets in the way. Therapists who call attention to what the patient *cannot* do only serve to amplify the difficulty while hiding the possibility.

Focusing on what a person is able to do builds a sense of competence. Within the context of this support, the person enters the process with a higher capacity for play and experimentation and with a minimum of ego involvement. Rapid recovery and a far more positive attitude result.

The holonomic model demands attention to wholeness and affirms the open-system nature of the mind. Mechanistic models favor the "take charge" and "get results" interventionist approaches common to behaviorism. Coming full cycle, we can see the difference between focusing on deficits as opposed to focusing on strengths. No other information could be more important to teachers or parents. The brain-mind system is designed to promote continuity, survival and holism.

I sense something strong and powerful that is acting with interior as well as exterior force.
Jonas Salk

Such is the basic premise of holonomy. Whether we are considering a person, a city or even a planet, we begin from the premise that each part is really an element of a larger whole. By ignoring that whole, we do disservice to the part and to the whole as well. In holonomy, the information gained from studying the parts is woven back into a larger and more inclusive perspective. The holistic premise, "yes and . . ." supersedes the more fragmented one, "yes but . . ."

Summary

All three models of brain-mind function offer insights into how the system works. We escape the confines of the mechanistic models with all three. The lateralized model affirms the presence of two major mind modalities—in itself enough to revolutionize education and provide more sensitivity during the early years of parenting. The triune model links us to the broad sweep of evolution. The holonomic model unites the concept of mind with the organizational models of matter, energy and the universe. The remarkable evolution in physics this last century has provided new perspectives in every field of science including the neurosciences. Holonomy testifies to a larger kind of unity, one close to the postulates of design.

The parenting and teaching approaches contained in *OPENMIND/WHOLEMIND* are based on the holonomic model. Its openness and completeness provide a viable foundation for transforming parenting and teaching. The reductivism and narrowness that formerly characterized human experience have served only to create and abet the problems we now face as individuals and as societies. It may well be that humankind is standing on its last threshold of survival, and that threshold has more to do with how we use our minds than with how much wealth and material resources we have. It may well be that *how we know* will emerge as more important than *what we believe*.

In a previous book, I defined holonomy as follows:

holonomy, holo·nomy n. (Gr. *holos*, entire, complete, whole and *nomos*, a law or rule. The science or systematic study of wholes, of entire systems, etc. Basic to holonomy is the simultaneous interrelatedness and interpenetration of all phenomena. Basic to holonomy is the assumption of unity and oneness as opposed to fragmentation, isolation and separateness.

Holonomic Assumptions about the Brain-Mind System

The holonomic model carries with it certain implications that are central to open-system theory. None of the earlier models of the brain-mind share this premise of openness. Whether we like it or not, our basic assumptions affect our willingness to try out new things ourselves and with our children. If our assumptions are closed, we are closed to experimentation and innovation.

For example. Let's assume that men are not supposed to show emotion. More specifically, that they are not supposed to allow their eyes to fill with tears, or even worse, cry in public. The effect of this assumption is to define manliness as supreme mastery over feelings and emotion. Such a definition denies or disregards the design that millions of years of evolution have produced. We *have* a limbic system, a brain stem, a cerebellum and a right hemisphere, all of which enable us to experience emotions ranging from terror and aggression to love and aesthetics. If we deny these design features, we deny our humanness as well.

Holonomy is a way of synthesizing the things we know about the brain-mind system. The assumptions that follow are based on extensive literature research; on implications inherent in my interpretation of the works of Karl Pribram, David Bohm and Ilya Prigogine; and on my own work with infants, pre-school and school-age children and adults in the areas of creativity, preconscious processes and dream state thought. Each assumption is a starting place for more formal exploration. The reader will detect some repetition from earlier pages; nevertheless, it is useful to present these assumptions in one listing.

Each of the assumptions that follow offers a series of expanding perspectives about the design of the brain-mind system. Each explores a facet of the open-system nature of the human mind.

Assumption 1: Each part of the brain-mind system experiences everything experienced by the other parts of the brain-mind system.

Early studies of the brain led us to believe that each brain-mind experience is localized in specific places in the brain. This is clearly not so. The whole brain is activated in the act of gaining experience. Although the brain is specialized for processing experience, such specialization does not invalidate this assumption. Inherent in this assumption is that the whole brain-mind system is the beneficiary of experience but the experience is processed or "sensed" in different ways.

How many times does the smell of new-mown hay or freshly baked bread bring a whole rush of images and memories to your consciousness—grandmother's house, a summer in Maine, a restaurant you visited after an alpine hike? Our brain-mind functions as a context—a pattern through time. Thus it remembers and associates things relationally. As we and our children accept this, we become more attentive to the limits of remembering and retrieving our experiences. When limiting edges overlap more and we can honor multiple modalities at once, we can learn to be more whole-minded.

Significance: This assumption prepares us to treat the brain-mind system as a whole instead of an aggregate of separate systems.

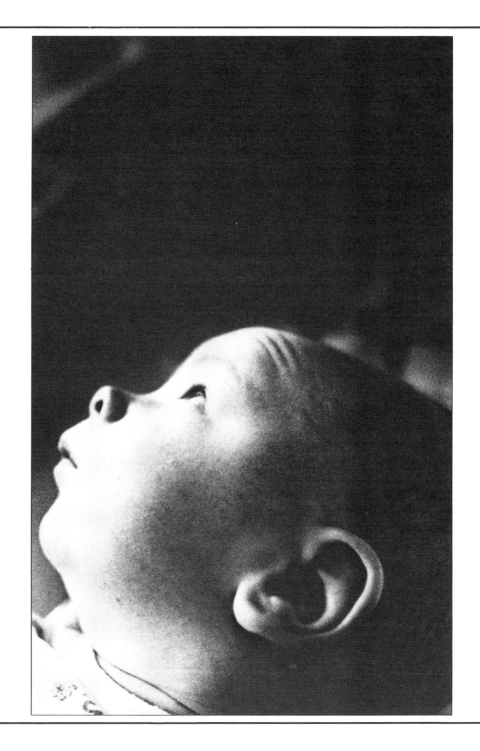

Assumption 2: Every part of the brain-mind system "knows" everything that every other part "knows."

Traditionally, researchers used electrical current to stimulate the brain in order to identify specific localized functions—what the brain supposedly "knew" in that place. These findings biased subsequent researchers, causing them to believe that these places were the only places where the brain "knew" that specific thing. Now, however, researchers working with people whose brains are damaged are discovering remarkable redundancy in how and where experience is encoded. Not only does the whole brain-mind seem to experience things, but experience is encoded in a variety of ways depending on the functions ordinarily performed.

Did you ever ask a child what color something was and have the child say, "elephant!" I did, and I knew at once what the child meant even though her teacher did not. I was reminded that elephant was *not* a substitute for *grey*. All that happened was the child selected a visual-verbal center instead of an abstract-verbal center to provide me with the "right" answer. I felt sure that, as the child grew in her ability to sort through her memory banks, she would get the specifically correct answer more frequently.

Significance: This assumption prepares us to realize that there are an immense number of ways we can get the brain-mind system to tell us what it "knows." If we do not get results in one way, we need to try another. (One of the tragedies of our time is how in parenting and schooling we stay focused on a narrow range of "appropriate" ways of harvesting the wisdom of the brain-mind system.)

We shape knowledge in the way we know it.
Michael Polanyi

Assumption 3: Humans can expand the range of what they pay attention to within their own brain-mind system.

Karl Pribram has said consciousness is what we pay attention to. In our culture, we consider a remarkably narrow range of mind functions appropriate. This narrowness is exaggerated in both parenting and teaching— many of the ways of "knowing" demonstrated by children are edited and censored at home and in school. As adults, we are reluctant to "pay attention" to unconventional things. Fortunately, the closedness we establish by such a "censored" history is reversible. We can reawaken ways of knowing long dormant. The popularity of visualization, meditation, dream reflection and other learned methods for "paying attention to" different expressions of consciousness testifies to this fact. Whether we acknowledge them or not, the nineteen senses we possess are providing input all the time. Much of what we call "expanded consciousness" is little more than re-learning to pay attention to our design.

Our son knows many more adults than he knows children. As a result he doesn't remember adults' names as well as he does children's names. He can harvest memories of people from his first year if I take the time to re-construct the context of a person's presence. I have to talk about food, weather, odors, the description of the house and the size of the person. Once I do that he can begin to supply many other details I had overlooked.

By intentionally sensing and recalling multiple attributes of experience, we expand our range of thinking, learning and knowing. In other words, we extend our consciousness to the true boundaries of experience.

Significance: The brain-mind system's acquired habits of closedness are reversible. We can teach children to harvest their experiences holistically and we can re-teach adults to utilize brain-mind patterns once thought lost.

Assumption 4: By increasing the number of brain-mind functions to which we pay attention, we extend consciousness and increase flexibility and fluency of mind function.

Increasing the number of functions to which we pay attention in the brain-mind system brings remarkable benefits. One of the foremost is a gain in self esteem and self image. This gain accompanies the realization that we have more options than we have taken advantage of. A second major benefit is in the area of problem solving. People who recognize more options are more likely to be more sensitive to unique choices available to them. Thus their solutions to problems are likely to be more lasting.

Therapists often tell us that mental illness is characterized by a pathological limitation of the ways we think. Narrowness also characterizes those who suffer what has been called "rational neurosis"— exaggeration of the processes of logical and reductive thought. By systematically using a variety of Learning Modalities (See Part IV.) we can increase the number of ways we can harvest experience. This process is called *flexibility* of thought. We can also increase our sophistication in each of these ways. This is called *fluency*. Flexibility and fluency are central to the mindwork of children. They can be reinstated and supported in adults.

A child was asked to draw a picture that had five balls in it. Her response was the following picture:

When the paper was returned the child was chagrined to find it marked wrong. When she asked about it the teacher said the correct answer was as shown below:

The child could never muster up the courage to defend her drawing. She had simply made the ball that described the "head" much larger than the four that designated the ears and eyes. The nose and smile were merely a bonus.

In childhood the cognitive process is essentially poetic.
Edith Cobb

Significance: Flexibility and fluency of thought can be enhanced through parenting and education.

Assumption 5: By honoring a wider variety of mind functions, we can increase the number of ways to express conventional functions.

Researchers have noted students' improved performance in reading, writing and arithmetic skills as a result of their developing visual, auditory and kinesthetic wisdom. My colleagues and I have demonstrated that increasing the diversity of brain-mind functions produces positive effects in personality and creativity as well as in physical and mental health.

I recall asking first-grade students to write sentences for me. Their worried looks warned me of the threat implicit in my assignment. I smiled and said to them, "What if you wanted to write the word *scary!*" They looked nervously at each other and then back at me. I had gone to the chalkboard and said, "Here is how I would write scary if I couldn't spell it . . ." This is what I drew:

I also told them this is how I would write automobile:

After a few more examples they went joyfully into my assignment. They knew they could intermix their writing skills with my "hieroglyphic" or "pictographic" style. Immediately they shared thoughts on paper far beyond their spelling abilities. In months to come the teacher perfected the techniques by always writing the words alongside the childrens' images. She thus bonded some of their visual, auditory, kinesthetic, emotional and spiritual expressions with the conventions of reading and writing.

Significance: The brain-mind system is designed to express what it knows in many ways. Forced inhibition or limiting of that range of expression creates the potential for illness and pathology. Conversely, sponsoring and nurturing diversity results in a natural tendency toward health and balance.

Assumption 6: We cannot avoid using our whole brain-mind system.

Contrary to the adage that we use only ten percent of our brains, neural activity is constant in distribution throughout our brain. Variations are in the intensity and quality of the activity. What is at issue is not whether the brain is *on*, but whether or not we are *paying attention to* what is *on*. Again the narrowness of our cultural experience is the dominant influence in regard to the focus and range of mind function. Since the system is always *on*, our task is to harvest effectively by learning to scan our choices with a greater sense of appropriateness and "fit."

An example I used earlier related to how many adults confess that they hate math. Upon questioning, however, we find that it's not math they dislike, but rather the rigor, absolute certainty and absence of a margin for error they experienced as they learned math.

In my own youth, I feared separation from my mother while she worked at a defense shipyard during 1942. I was eight, fatherless and thrust into a drab, grey, uninspired version of daycare that was far more prisonlike than homelike. I was served oatmeal with raisins in it twice a day. It was hot for breakfast and cold at lunch. During cooking, the raisins would bloat up to look like rotten grapes. My brainstem, limbic system and cortex were all active. I was taught many lessons about patriotism, personal hygiene and how to help others during those days. But whatever went into my cortex was overwhelmed by how fearful I was. I thought we would be bombed and my mother killed while welding in the dark bowels of a troopship.

As teachers and parents, we cannot assume that what we teach subsumes all experience. We cannot teach addition to a child who's afraid there's a spider in the desk. For lasting progress, we have to legitimize and create comfort about what's in the mind *and* what's in the desk.

Significance: Responsibility for the completeness with which we harvest our minds rests with each of us. And, as parents and teachers, we must assume responsibility for the degree to which we encourage children's access to their minds.

Assumption 7: The brain-mind system retains all experience.

This assumption is the most controversial so far because it contradicts the entrenched view that we become insane if we remember all that we experience. Several theorists have devised remarkable processes by which the brain supposedly filters perception and recall so that there is a minimum of overload. I am not denying that we have neural "referees" in our recall process; Kubie's hypnotic recall experiments show that we do. I am saying that we can have monitors on our recall capability at the same time we encode all experience in memory.

Significance: This assumption allows us to proceed as though memory-harvesting is a trainable skill that may be enhanced by trusting and attending to a greater number of different things.

The next three assumptions, best called theoretical faiths, are based on writings at the growing edge of contemporary science; works of Capra, Sheldrake, Pribram, Bohm and Prigogine are central to their inclusion.

Assumption 8: The brain-mind system is an open system. Its patterns of functioning can be originated from within and may be configured from without.

A mind can think by itself and it can be taught. This means a mind is both inside and outside Fuller's circle. This fits if we envision students and teachers or parents and children "mindworking" together. As long as all parties adhere to cultural convention little is of concern. When experiences not within the accepted cultural limits begin to pattern mind expression, however, the shadows fall on credibility. The entire realm of parapsychological phenomena is enfranchised with this assumption. Spiritual visions and profound insights are potential outcomes.

The phone rings and, coincidence upon coincidence, it is the person you have just been thinking about. Or having decided on a career move, you call a new company to find out if they have any openings in your field. The division head takes your call moments after an employee resigns. These are common events, in everyday life. They are far more common than we realize because they usually have to be dramatically thrust upon us before we notice them.

With so many available senses (nineteen perhaps), could it be possible for us to learn to tune in to more subtle messages? Can we admit that if we have nineteen senses and thus at least as many modalities for accessing and expressing experience, we are *designed* to know and learn in inexplicable ways?

Significance: This assumption removes the final block inherent in the traditional Western models of brain-mind design—the notion that logic and rationality are the mind's only valid thought forms. Reductive analysis is deemed necessary to produce rational solutions to problems and rational bases for knowledge. In effect, the Western model assumes the existence of reality upon which one day we all will "objectively" agree. The Western model treats the brain-mind as a closed system that acts upon the universe, not as a product of the universe. Western tradition places the brain-mind *inside* Fuller's circle.

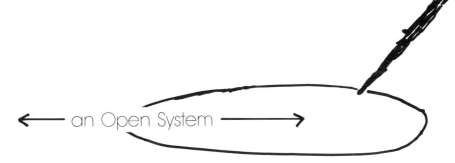

If the brain-mind is an open system, then it is also intimate with what lies outside the circle.

This means the brain-mind can change itself to adjust to external input. Sometimes it changes in response to sources *not* explainable by rational reductivism. When the brain-mind does this, it is usually explained as intuition and the processes we call intuitive leaps. Intuition represents the times when the mind leaps beyond the data, beyond the known sensory input and yields to patterns unknown. Western fear of such mind-work has resulted in our denial of such happenings.

Significance: An open-system relationship exists between thought and its source, whether that source is internal or external.

Assumption 9: The brain-mind system is what unites the person with the universe.

Holonomy is the systematic study of wholes, of entireties. As such, holonomy presumes a unity in form, function and design. Because the brain-mind is holonomic, it is part of the form, the function and design of the universe. The fragmentation inherent in Western thought has prevented our recognition of this unity.

Yet we have benefitted. Western science, particularly physics, has pushed reductivism to its limits. Its division of matter into its compound parts has thrust a new reality upon our consciousness. The new reality proposes a unity between matter and energy—it suggests that matter is patterned energy. As surely as the brain-mind is made of matter, so too is the universe. We have given ourselves permission to recognize the all-pervasive unity that binds us.

The cover of this book captures such a moment of recognition. Our son was midway through his second year and we had gone into a wondrous forest in the California coastal range. He walked with confidence into a leafy bower. I sat apart with a long lens on my camera and photographed him as he emerged from behind his newly-found friends—the trees and shrubs. Somehow I knew he knew them. He showed absolutely no fear at being separate from me. If anything, he had looked up to assure himself that *I* was all right.

His immersion was one of unity—he was using his brain-mind to the fullness of its design. On some future date he may relate in words what was etched on his soul that day. I may never know. But the mystery of it all is captured in this backward glance, a glance back to genetic memory—his and the planet's.

Significance: This assumption unifies the assumptions that precede it.

Assumption 10: In open-system unity there exists a capacity for harmonious evolution.

The unity of the brain-mind is driven by evolutionary processes. The changes which result are manifested in form, function and design. Evolution has created a panorama of change that has resulted in all that exists on our planet and all that can be found in the universe.

Erich Jantsch once glibly remarked that "the universe must be a primary example of evolutionary continuity since it is still here after twenty billion years." In a more reflective vein this notion seems true. Evolution presents us with a symphony of success. The contemporary is a concert of continuity from eons past.

The dominant consciousness brought forward by evolution embraces change which leads toward success. The universe seems to have become what it is, via billions of trials and billions of errors, all guided by a tendency toward harmonious, evolving continuity.

The most urgent need today is to restore the magic powers of love, confidence and belief in the perfectability of humankind.
Robert Muller

Significance: The human brain-mind and the very fabric of the universe are pledged to each other by the grand sweep of evolution. All that our minds can do is part of this process—and we can assist its benevolence by guiding our own consciousness. In other words, we can begin to guide our own ways of thinking to reflect processes that are in harmony with evolutionary continuity.

The brain, a four-pound pinkish-grey mass on a laboratory table. But when that brain is in concert with a living, growing being, it is a miracle of possibilities. Mind gives the magic to a setting.

Do these assumptions limit or liberate us? Do we have more or fewer options if each is valid? If I accept and act on these, will I sacrifice any grace the children before me possess? Can I add to their graces? For me the answer is clear. To pledge our minds toward continuity, and to honor the same possibilities within our children's minds, is the journeywork of the universe.

Mind is the child of the universe . . . it is the medium of understanding, enchantment and reason that all beings share.

The Holonomic Model in Parenting and Education

The implications of the holonomic model for education and parenting are profound. However, most of us have not experienced much holonomy in our educations and, for some, very little in our parenting. We are the children of a reductive paradigm. We were born into the great flowering of the industrial revolution. The revolution had all but died, but the flowering continued. We became a people with unmatched access to material goods and striving for what we called a high standard of living. Yet with all the remarkable social and economic changes we experienced precious little change in our world view. We clung to the idea that school made one "smart," with smartness being defined by the three Rs and reductive thought. We were committed to the idea that following the rules, whether written or not, was the way to get along.

Recall our models of mind. The closed-system mind necessitated narrowness and reductive approaches because it could not harbor contradictions. Education as well as parenting required the "answers," "truth," the "right" way and closure. In the open-system mind, openness, tentativeness, multiple possibilities, appropriateness and ambiguity may comfortably be entertained while one explores ideas.

Whether provided by parenting or education, the closed-system mind prepares one to reflexively rush to convention for answers. If it expresses originality, it is an expression of elegance in conventional wisdom. The open mind, while not denying convention, uses it as a starting place for original exploration. Its conclusions most often draw convention into a more realistic balance with the nature of changing times. Thus the open mind expresses originality as creativity—a transformational context.

A predisposition toward closedness and reductive models in parenting and education limits the number of options a child can experience. Moreover it limits them in the direction of convention and conformity. A predisposition toward openness and holonomic models results in increased options for the child. It permits grounding in convention but treats conformity as an option not a requirement.

Society limited options in the past to ensure predictability and stability. Now that the rules are changing in our open, information-abundant society, many are not able to cope. Responding to the profusion of options that present themselves in daily life is not easy. We are compelled to make choices independently of social convention. Do we run and hide in the conventions of history or do we, as parents and educators, accept our responsibilities and help today's children move beyond hesitation and into the world of the future?

Ken Peterson, a professor of education at the University of Utah, is one of the finest teachers I have ever met. He once told me, "Teaching is easy if you assume that each student already knows all he or she needs to know to be here." At first I took this as a glib witticism. Now this idea is the basis of a holonomic world view. To Ken, teaching is celebrating a student's already-rich resources and seeking new domains of wisdom.

Ken seems to accept inherently the notion that the brain-mind system was designed to work. Moreover, he seems convinced that students enjoy the experience of having that system work. His teaching methods guide his students' self-discovery of both aesthetics and reason. When he looks at a student, Ken sees learning assets rather than disabilities. His approach falls in line with Pribram's findings, discussed earlier, regarding the recovery "teaching" of patients who have lost certain mind functions due to surgery or other traumas.

In the neurosciences, holonomic approaches yield remarkable results. In education, a growing force of pioneering teachers are demonstrating that such approaches also are compatible with classroom instruction. Both fields are producing evidence that optimal learning occurs when the entire brain-mind system is involved.

If we accept at all the validity of the holonomic model, the most important single notion that should be stressed is the notion of the wholeness of the mind. *We must approach children as though their minds are complete, intact and functioning.* An infant is not devoid of wisdom and experience just because he or she does not possess the language to express it. A child of two, listening to discourse between his or her parents, cannot be thought to be uncomprehending simply because he or she does not enter into the conversation. A child who never knows the answer in mathematics cannot honestly be labelled a "non-learner." If nothing else, the child may well have learned to dislike mathematics.

The brain-mind cannot *not* learn. In the past, parents and teachers have judged a child's learning on the basis of what *they* wanted children to learn. The child, on the other hand, is just interested in learning. While teachers focus on math, children may well respond by creating ways to avoid embarrassment and humiliation. The child fails if math skills are the sole criterion of success, but succeeds if learning includes how to avoid emotional pain.

The above child is being forced into a closed system—the system of hating and avoiding math. In standard closed-system approaches, the teacher persists by assigning more math. Using holonomic methods, the teacher would investigate the fear that caused the child's embarrassment and humiliation. Neither teacher nor parent can reach the cortex when the child's brain stem and limbic system are scurrying for safety.

Elation is the child's generic response to the surrounding world.
Edith Cobb

Holonomic methods honor the entire brain. Holonomic approaches begin at once to confirm for children that they know a great deal about mathematics. But they "know" in different ways. Some need non-symbol images, such as a quantity of apples or oranges. Others need certain kinds of auditory input like music or even the tapping of a pencil on the desk. Others need to manipulate objects such as marbles or cubes. As these ways are established for the child, math becomes a new aesthetic of a holistic wisdom.

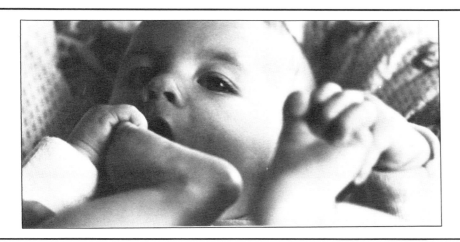

An infant is not devoid of
wisdom and experience just
because he or she does
not possess the language to
express it.

When closed-system approaches are used to teach math, an adversarial role is often set up in a learner's mind. Learners begin to defend themselves with statements such as, "I hate math" and "Math is stupid." They eventually come to believe such explanations, effectively creating a closed-minded perception of math.

Closed-minded attitudes stem from positive beliefs as well. If someone solves a problem or gains a beneficial insight, he or she may note the mental processes followed and arrive at a "reason" for the success. Entering new situations such people believe they already know how to solve the problem. In holonomic approaches, beliefs do not filter experience.

Karl Pribram tells the story of how he was once called long distance to treat a young girl with a serious head injury. It took several hours for him to reach the patient and her condition had deteriorated seriously. Her head was swathed in bloodsoaked bandages and she was hardly breathing. Using his usual protocol he spoke to the apparently unconscious girl and said, "Hello, Cathy." She startled him by responding with, "Hello, Doctor." He was amazed that she was conscious.

Pribram instantly shifted his perspective. He did a rapid check of her neurological characteristics and discovered them to be normal. As he checked her further he found several broken ribs puncturing her lung. *This was the real cause of her trauma.*

This is a perfect example of how conception can cloud and interfere with perception. The physician who made the original diagnosis had focused on the apparent head injury; satisfied with that diagnosis, he had allowed three or four hours to pass while the patient slipped toward possible death.

The drama of medical diagnosis is often diluted when taken from the domain of the surgeons and the emergencies they face. Outside the operating room, diagnosis often seems trivial or offhand. Consider the number of times you have heard, "Her problem is. . ." or, "What he really needs is. . . ." Even more innocent are the categories or boxes into which we put the diagnosed. How many of us use diagnostic categories such as these: "terrible twos," "hyperactive," "shy," "just like his father," "slow," "slow learner," "non-reader," "clumsy," "non-artistic?"

Each of these descriptors, when accepted as true, becomes a limiting condition, a self-fulfilling prophecy. How many women who as children were affectionately labeled "non-mechanical" later made a lifestyle out of being unable to fix things or deal with mechanical tasks. Such labels or descriptors reduce a person's options and lead to a lifetime of closed-system experiences.

As mentioned earlier, R. Buckminster Fuller was fond of saying that his education was an exercise in surviving misinformation. Bucky found it easy to transcend convention, but he lamented that others lacking the ability to cast off what had been mis-taught would live with garlands of falsehoods draping their perception. The greatest liability of knowing the *truth* is that its embodiment in one's mind keeps one from verifying and testing it. It was "true" ten years ago that only radiation, chemotherapy and surgery could cure cancer. Today these methods still work, but so apparently do diet, attitude, visualization and changes in lifestyle.

As far as mind-function is concerned, our "Western" preference for reductive functions is culturally mandated. Our tendency toward holism is a response to natural design. In a sense, we are exploring the degree to which we allow our enculturation to imprison us. Other cultures have a far wider perspective of acceptable mind-function. The tribal cultures of North America and many of the southern hemisphere accept ways of knowing that are unacceptable under the glaring scrutiny of Western thought. Whereas tribal societies seek out and respect people who draw on mystical and super-spiritual ways of knowing, we institutionalize them. The tribal people consider these unexplainable mental gifts worthy of honor and support.

When I come into the presence of a child who thinks differently and "knows" differently, I try to settle into that child's mode of knowing. I must rekindle or learn anew what it is the child experiences.

If I force the child to see the world in the narrow patterns of my history and my perspectives, I lose the opportunity to be a true teacher.

Consider the following: Midway through our son's third year, we decided to return to the Rocky Mountains to live. Colorado had been my primary childhood home. My wife Cheryl and I had met there, and it seemed like home to her as well. Circumstances were such that on our first trip there to find a new home, Cheryl and I could not leave the same day. So I packed for Stician and myself and we set out for Colorado. I had called ahead and arranged for a close and long-time friend to meet us at the airport. Bonnie had been excited about our return to Colorado and we talked incessantly on the drive from Denver to Boulder. Sticie slept in the back seat.

As we approached the city limits of Boulder, Sticie sat up stiffly in the back seat. His voice startled us both as it was strangely bold. We were rising upon the overpass that crossed Baseline Street near the University. Sticie pointed out the window and said sharply, "That's where I lived when I used to work here."

I turned and saw he was pointing to the east. I was confused and asked him to repeat what he had said. "That's where I lived when I used to work here." He was pointing to the apartment building in which I had lived five years before his birth. By this time Bonnie, who had known me then, was wide-eyed. I touched her shoulder to calm her and asked Stician to describe the building he meant. He said, "The big white one with the red roof."

Again I settled my own excitement and cast a bewildered look at Bonnie. By now we were both amazed, but I managed a tone of voice that seemed normal and calm. This was, after all, the exact building where I had lived—and yet this was our son's first trip to Boulder, and he was pointing directly at it. I decided on the clincher. "What color were the carpets when you lived there?" "*Red*," he shouted. " they were bright red!"

"That's great," I said, and we drove on, trying not to be excited in the way that frightens or embarrasses children. It was difficult, but Bonnie and I managed to express a complete acceptance of the event. We didn't want to do what many would do and call undue attention to Sticie's vision and perception. I had known many children who gave up such ways of knowing when they found they created a stir among adults.

The carpet *was* red and that *had* been the building in which I had lived. Had Sticie discovered this by overhearing an idle conversation? Was it coincidence? I quickly ruled out these possibilities. I don't usually talk about apartments and rugs. I most certainly didn't coach the child on the location of a years old home in a city he had never visited. I did not wake him in the back seat, and Bonnie and I were talking about new homes—not old ones.

In the holonomic model of the brain-mind system, *all* functions of mind are accepted as legitimate. The brain-mind is an open system in such a perspective and thus is open to input and experience from without as well as within. The ways of knowing we used to call parapsychology may well turn out to be completely "normal." As we entertain the consequences of these models, we may come to realize that we do not really know what *normal* is.

Children never give a wrong answer. . . .they merely answer a different question. It is our job to find out which one they answered correctly and honor what they know.

M.I.S.C.: MODALITIES, INTELLIGENCES, STYLES, AND CREATIVITY

PART IV

Introduction

Living is an exercise in learning. Of the hundreds of events that weave a day together, each is capable of extending our ability to know more about ourselves and the world. Often we believe that only certain of these events are true learning situations, while others are merely part of day-to-day living, hardly worthy of attention let alone mention. Yet some people view every thing that happens as an opportunity to learn. They seek meaning in all kinds of experience and never drift in the doldrums of routine.

In his fascinating book, *The Human Cycle*, Colin Turnbull says,

> All around us, at every moment in our lives, reaching out and touching us, there is a world of excitement and fascination. Its riches are denied to none, for beauty and wonder lie at every stage of the life cycle, from childhood to old age, transforming poverty into wealth, squalor into magnificence, tedium into sport, fear into recognition, hatred and bigotry into understanding. Access to this world does not require any great feat of intellect, nor does it demand a lifetime dedicated to the quest. All that is needed is a mind and a soul, the soul being that which opens the mind, breathing life into it, making it infinitely curious. The senses that are common to all of us, regardless of who or what we are, provide us with all the tools we need. [4]

Turnbull is describing the way we enter the world. Before we can walk, talk, or write, we are filled with the ecstasy of learning.

Seldom do we see infants lost in boredom. For them, the world and each minute in it are filled with wonder and enchantment. They can watch, in fascination, a patch of light creep across the wall above their crib. Sometimes they'll spend hours in careful examination of their fingers or a corner of the blanket that covers them.

Adults who retain this inherent fascination or sense of wonder about the world have no "special" times for learning. They are the ones who preserve the childlike qualities of the great creators of history, for whom life itself is the ultimate forum for learning.

Unfortunately, there are many who believe otherwise. For such people, learning takes place primarily in formal, structured or institutional settings. Schools or colleges, churches, books, seminars, training sessions and experts are the established channels through which "acceptable" learning takes place. The self and personal experience are not regarded as valid sources.

Sometime past mid-life, many people experience a reawakening of self. Reacting against years of self-denial, they return to the joy and excitement of personal discovery and growth. Calling this period a "mid-life crisis," popular authors have made it a status symbol of adult development.

For some, this "crisis" has become a way to break with narrow lifestyles, to shuck the societal restrictions that have engendered a gnawing sense of emptiness. Lacking the courage to break free of these restrictions, they invent a crisis in the form of divorce, career change, or even a "nervous breakdown." All represent ways of lashing back at a lifetime of subservience to the external.

The drama of a crisis has the effect of excusing them from living up to societal norms. If the crisis is severe enough, they can re-enter life in an "Act Two" status, sometimes evading the hard work of self-examination and determination of a life's purpose.

My guess is that the "crisis" status of this time of reawakening is both overstated and unnecessary. Such a turning point perhaps is a crisis only when we cling to the cultural and social myths that have estranged us from self-guided learning in the first place.

Quiet, non-dramatic shifts can mark equally remarkable changes in lifestyle. The antidote for a crisis-based lifestyle change is a change in consciousness. Consciousness, you may recall, was defined as *what we pay attention to*.

Am I claiming that something as traumatic as a mid-life crisis (or any other kind of personal tragedy) is not a prerequisite to a shake-up in lifestyle? The answer is an emphatic *Yes!* Tragedy and misfortune are not *necessary* conditions for major life changes.

Central to all this is the concept of the open mind. Options and alternatives are the lifeblood of learning and growth throughout life. The closed mind turns options into dogma which can be dismantled *only* through a major effort. Such a destruction of belief can hardly be called anything other than "crisis."

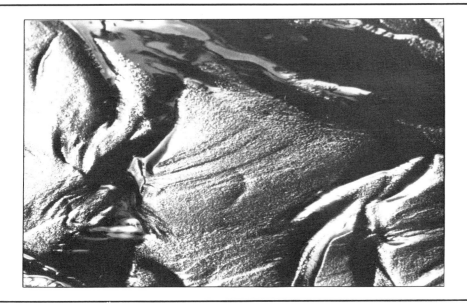

The earth is our first teacher.

There are elements of dogma in the day-to-day which in effect structure our perceptions of the options available to us. Psychologists argue that we will probably parent and teach in the ways we have been parented and taught. What this means is that the options that were available to our parents and teachers are the ones we will offer to our children. There is little in research to refute this established pattern. The studies of child abuse present ghastly data to support it. If we were abused as children it is likely that we will abuse our children. Food, clothing and even automobile preferences can be traced back into family history.

Forming habits is raised to an art form in school. This first formal setting for learning substantially influences a child's perception and conception of what learning is. Teaching methods, school materials, the rules of demeanor and the systems of evaluation are all party to learning closedness in schools.

Nurturing change in schools seemed a low priority for both educators and parents for a long time. But resistance to change is weakening. Perhaps it is weakening for the same reasons that mid-life crises are no longer necessary for making lifestyle changes. Like parents, teachers are also bathed in the transforming consciousness of the times. In spite of a renewal of concern for "the basics" and schoolwork, educators are addressing their obligation to lifework. They are preparing students for the tentativeness of the future. More and more, holism is the key that promises success as educators close the door on 19th century instructional theories and practices.

Joy in looking and comprehending is nature's most beautiful gift.
Albert Einstein

We started this discussion with some commentary on the rigidity of past habits of thought and behavior. The example of the mid-life crisis—just one of many that could have been used—personalized the sometimes imprisoning effects of closed systems. The purpose of this book so far has been to counteract this inexorable movement toward the closed mind.

At this juncture, we will continue to examine ways to facilitate the journey toward the honoring of our genetic mandate. . . the openness of the brain-mind system. Most promising among these are the approaches arising out of the study of learning modalities, multiple intelligences, learning styles and creativity.

These approaches are based on current brain-mind research and years of application. They apply to learners of all ages. My colleagues and I have used these approaches in retirement communities, colleges and universities and all levels of schooling for young people. In addition, we have used them to train managers in industry, the military, public administration and in dozens of other professions.

In the opening chapter I introduced the acronym M.I.S.C. This stands for Modalities, Intelligences, Styles (learning styles) and Creativity. The remainder of *OPENMIND/WHOLEMIND* analyzes these concepts and presents practical methods based on M.I.S.C. for systematically monitoring our patterns relating to children. M.I.S.C. represents an "awareness checklist" for parents or teachers to enable them to determine how completely they are honoring childrens' capabilities.

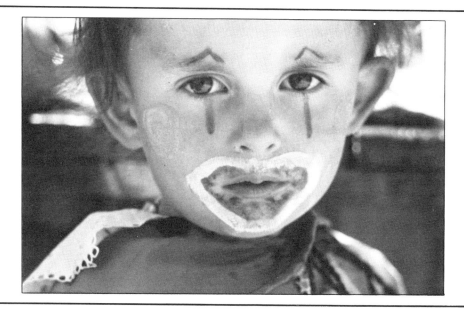

Although *OPENMIND/WHOLEMIND* is about parenting and teaching, its fundamental premises have been proven in the fields of education, management, government, theology, military, science, medicine and in the service professions. Self-imposed narrowness penalizes everyone; we can truly benefit from becoming more open. This book helps us extend options to children and also to ourselves.

Learning Modalities

Learning modalities are an expression of the design of the brain-mind system. They represent our fundamental capacities to gain and create experience. Learning modalities are the variety of ways in which the brain-mind system accesses experience (input) and expresses experience (output). All our learning modalities are linked to our senses. The majority are direct links; a few are representations of what we experience translated into the form of abstractions. Remarkably, our design allows us to substitute symbol codes for sensory experience in both input and output. Although never as rich, symbol codes do allow us this vicarious experience. Abstract symbols have come to be the tool box of the senses. We use abstract symbols to substitute for sensory experience.

The modalities are the brain-mind system's access routes to the world. In addition to gathering experience through the senses, the modalities govern the ways experience can be expressed through communication. Recall that we have nineteen senses, fourteen more than the five we usually acknowledge. Clearly there are modalities for input and output within each of those senses—senses we generally ignore. This means we experience both input and output that generally go unrecognized.

The real purpose in studying learning modalities is to expand possibilities. Learners can address the ways they have come to limit the use of their own modalities—they can consciously rehearse new ways of thinking. This is true in both school and life.

By using what we know about learning modalities, we can orchestrate an intentional variety in the experiences offered to children. They gain a richer and more flexible repertoire of ways to participate in an ever-changing world. We should strive to establish the integrity of both metaphoric and rational thought and teach children to honor the breadth of mind. In addition we must hone specific reductive skills as well. This is the primary purpose of the learning modality activities presented in Part V of this book.

In homes and schools where the inherent value of the learning modalities is not recognized, there is an unbridled rush toward force-feeding children a narrow range of skills. Parents often try to load children's experiences with the three Rs and so-called critical thinking skills in the hopes of raising them to the dubious status of "super kids." The children's formerly wide range of modalities atrophies as they try to accommodate this narrow definition of talents. The outcome is a tragedy.

We diminish children's confidence and measure their worth narrowly. Parents and teachers who acknowledge and develop a limited suite of skills are inadvertently ensuring our unpreparedness to address the future. Today's adults stand in testimony to schools and a society that have denied our full capacities. The anguish of our own lack of wholeness—parent against child, citizen against citizen, nation against nation—is a manifestation of the cruel limits we have enforced upon ourselves and others. To the extent that we honor and nurture whole human beings, ours will be a more peaceful planet. Developing the modalities promises to increase our children's life skills as well as our own.

I focus on five major categories of learning modalities: Symbolic-Abstract, Visual, Kinesthetic, Auditory and Synergic. These are the modalities that are most appropriate to school, family, and corporate settings. These are the modalities which have been researched most thoroughly by neuroscientists. Even the most conservative school administrator cannot refute their significance to teaching (whereas some will argue about the relevance of other modalities, such as taste, smell, pheromones and eidetic imagery!).

By including use of these modalities in lesson plans in school and in playful explorations with children at home (Part V), we create experiences that gradually awaken them to the design capabilities of their brain-mind system. We help children learn to respect each modality's unique contribution to wholeness in knowing. To ignore any one in parenting and teaching is increasingly inexcusable. Each person is uniquely endowed. Our role is to orchestrate the means and nurture the courage to answer the call of our design.

Symbolic-Abstract

Few cultures so religiously adhere to the Symbolic-Abstract modalities as do the technologically-sophisticated ones. We have a unique love affair with abstract codes. We judge a person's intelligence on how skillfully he or she uses them. They have become our primary means of communication, and many teachers and parents see the major function of schooling as the imparting of reading, writing and ciphering skills.

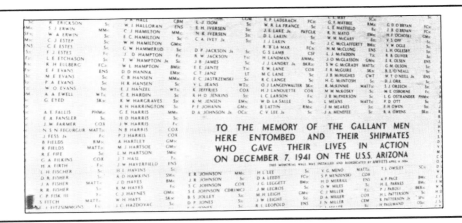

Codes are representations—they stand for some form of reality. We use an "A" for excellence in schools, a "1" for the best in sports, a 280ZX for the model of a car and even a 3.1417 for the relationship between the radius of a circle and its circumference. We express reality in symbols such as a, b, c, d, e, or 1, 2, 3, 4, 5. More specialized symbols take the forms of α β γ, ? & $ %, $\geq \leq \sqsubset\!\supset$. The most important things about symbols and codes are often forgotten in their teaching and use: they stand *for* reality, they are not reality.

All codes and the symbols that express them are governed by rational, logical, sequential and time-ordered rules, the so-called "left-brained" forms of processing. The words you are now reading follow the rules of standardized spelling. Misspelled words stand out (if you learned your lessons well). We are even more disciplined in our allegiance to rules for expressing numbers. Numbers are the emblems of exactness. With words we can say "a few geese" or a "herd of elephants." But the exactness that accompanies the descriptions, "3 geese" and "29 elephants," is unmatched.

Another unique characteristic of symbolic mindwork is that the symbols inevitably take on their own meaning. The mind begins to manipulate them for their own sake and forgets that they were created for representation purposes. For many, this function of the mind is the most glamorous. It becomes the "great game in the mind." Exploring the intricacies of thought through the manipulation of symbols is a seduction few can resist. In a very real sense, this is the world represented best by psychologist Jean Piaget's Formal Operations stage of thought. That stage of thought is best served by symbols and abstract codes, since it involves reasoning about things you haven't experienced.

When children become skilled in Symbolic-Abstract modalities, they invariably are labelled bright or intelligent. Thus many parents rigorously attend to their children's attempts at reading and writing. Their preschoolers learn to count to ten and recite the alphabet. "Sesame Street" and other forms of television instruction have extended early symbol training to nearly all children, creating a democratization of access to Symbolic-Abstract functions.

Symbolic-Abstract functions are so prized in our society we would be irresponsible not to develop them in the educational process. They are useful. What we must avoid is the casting of these skills as the only ones appropriate to a discussion or description of human worth.

Visual

Visual wisdom arising from sight and binocular vision preceded human use of fire. It was the advantage that led to upright stance and to the use of tools and weapons; it was the capability that first urged us to create representative images. The first drawings on cave walls and clay tablets were the beginnings of writing and mathematics. Humans learned they could code experience in ways other than speech.

Humans found that what they saw and what they conceived were related yet separate. The role of vision was worthy enough in daily life, but also bestowed the capacity to record, implement and even transform what they had experienced. Art was the origin of mythic and religious notation. It helped early humans reach out to and communicate spiritually with the unknown.

Scholars who study the origins of written language nearly all agree that the first attempts at writing were pictures or pictographs. All written codes can be traced to representational artwork. The visual expression of what was later to be written-symbolic language is still alive in the Japanese Kanji ideographs originally derived from the Chinese. Research has shown that the Japanese people today process the "art-like" forms of the Kanji in the right hemisphere of the brain.

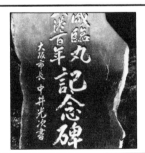

Children develop visual wisdom long before they acquire the wisdom of the Abstract-Symbolic code. Because modern parents and teachers are relatively insensitive to the sensory modalities (Visual, Kinesthetic and Auditory), they often ignore them or relegate them to support status in the quest for polished performance in reading, writing and arithmetic. Ironically, use of the sensory modalities can help achieve polished performance in such areas conventionally associated with the Symbolic-Abstract.

The Visual modalities are among the first a child utilizes to make sense in the world outside the womb. Infants as young as nine days have shown shifts in cortical processing as a result of repeated visual stimuli. The first expressions of logical ordering by the infant brain are shown in the shift from a right-hemisphere processing of a flashing light to a left-hemisphere response as the child creates a "logic" to the flashes.

Until recently, remarkably few educators have defended the value of visual wisdom outside the realm of the arts. Strangely, in many cultures, particularly European and some Asian societies, art has become a closed-system arena of human experience. It has taken on "rules" and is approached as content rather than process. Many of the foremost defenders of art as basic human experience, such as John Dewey, Rudolph Steiner and Carl Jung, have argued that we should preserve art as process as well as content.

Researchers have demonstrated that there is a differentiated processing of the brain's cortical hemispheres. Varying parts of the brain are activated by different conditions in processing experiences. Visual experience activates large banks of cortical cells all but ignored during the processing of abstract symbols. These visually-activated areas are not just sensory links, but possess a system of intellect of their own. By living in an environment where Visual modalities are nurtured and honored, children can develop sophistication in visual-spatial intelligences such as navigation, tracking and artistic expression. Data indicate that a systematic honoring of the visual forms of wisdom results in improved performance in Symbolic-Abstract modalities as well.

Anthropologists such as Margaret Mead and Colin Turnbull, as well as Native Americans Jamake Highwater and Vine Deloria, have expanded our perspective concerning sensory intelligence. The syntheses in psychologist Howard Gardner's *Frames of Mind* and my books, *Metaphoric Mind* and *Mind of Our Mother*, argue that rational perspectives are narrow and have reached a natural limit. We are now returning to an acknowledgement of the wider reaches of the brain-mind system. We are re-accessing our own design.

Visual wisdom is more than "art." *Visual wisdom is the parent of an intimate form of logic that depends upon metaphor as its structure.* Metaphor enhances meaning by linking large networks of unrelated experience. Facts and specific terms isolate and delimit meaning. Metaphor, particularly visual metaphor, is an *inclusive* and *proliferative* form of organizing experience. What this means is that *visual wisdom* is inherently connective and *creates mind-sets tending toward synthesis.* In everyday terms it creates a predisposition to the "big picture" ability to sense the forest rather than the trees. The metaphoric role of visual wisdom is shown often in Inuit or Eskimo carvings. Researchers commonly find carvings that represent two or more animals in the same body. The Inuit artist defends the sculpture by saying, "These were all in my mind, so I had to bring them out of the stone as well." The logic of connectedness rather than the logic of separation characterizes visual wisdom.

I am becoming more and more convinced that visual wisdom predisposes one to a more holistic world view than does symbolic wisdom. This is not to say that those with high symbolic abilities are devoid of holistic vision. Luminaries like R. Buckminster Fuller, Albert Einstein and Margaret Mead were all holistic visionaries. Many who develop holism as a world view are greeted by colleagues as adversaries or even deviates. Unfortunatly romanticism has been linked to such adversity and provides many with the excuse to "suffer" and feign oppression. Such indulgences must be carefully noted and best be abandoned as we parent and teach our children. Parenting and schooling may better be cast as an enterprise where visual wisdom and the entire evolutionary heritage of our brain-mind system are honored and celebrated.

Kinesthetic

Until recently the idea that the body represents the antithesis of mind has been imbedded in Western culture. We have been taught for more than two thousand years that our bodies are vehicles for sensory excess. Our bodies have been well-hidden by European and northern Asian clothing styles, and cultural rules have established carefully-monitored patterns of movement. Etiquette created hierarchies of appropriate repression.

The podium and the pulpit both hide the body from the audience. Academic and clerical robes were undoubtedly designed for the same purposes. In traditional schools, children are placed in immovable seats and are taught to face forward and fold their hands. If allowed to stand, they must stand in line facing in one direction. Teaching also reflects a uniform containment of the body: movement is to and from the seats and chalkboard, writing is standardized via the Palmer method of handwriting and names always appear in the upper right-hand corner of the paper. And speaking of handedness, the right hand does all the "right" things.

The military stringently disciplines the body in marching and in other posturings, such as "attention," "at ease" and "parade rest." Ironically, the military has presumed a unity between body and mind and used it for its own ends. It believes that if the body is trained, the mind will follow. Although this approach, respectful of body wisdom, is not at all what we will be exploring, it does represent a highly pragmatic expression of mind-body unity.

Another perhaps more enlightened arena of mind-body unity is found in the martial arts. Some of the martial arts date back hundreds if not thousands of years. Each begins with the assumption of mind-body unity. In all forms of martial art, one harmonizes the mind and the body in the performance of movement, dance, meditation, sensing, breathing and knowing.

In hundreds of classrooms across the country teachers and students are inviting the body into full partnership with the mind in learning. These are people who have learned to rekindle the childhood vitality felt when they learned to walk. They are restoring a "full being" kind of awareness and understanding, like that experienced with our first steps. Pioneering explorers of kinesthetic wisdom in education and parenting include Dianne Battung, Jake Nice, Susan Miller and Tom Walters. These and other distinctive educators recognize differences between dance as a classic art form, and how movement is involved in body wisdom.

Classical dance forms are often as kinesthetically rigid and constrained as Latin grammar. Students of such classical forms learn more about closed-system movement than about dance. Conversely, Native Indian dances, as well as those of other primal people, link the dancer with processes in nature and spirit. Western dance is linked to form and sequence. I recall all too well the tragedy in my life when my grandfather tried to teach me Slavic folk dances. This episode, designed to enlighten me about my heritage, deteriorated into a shambles. I seemed unable to get my feet to repeat the sequences grandfather had demonstrated. Finally this normally pleasant and loving man shouted, "Goddamit Boobya! Deese foots go right here and no pletz else—do it like I tell you!" His reddened face and thickening anger tore into the fear centers of my limbic and brain stem regions and ended my dance career on the spot. It was clear that my grandfather represented the structure of his heritage and not the joy of movement.

Kinesthetic wisdom is more than dance. Dance is a special case of kinesthetic wisdom, but so too are catching a fly ball, skiing, sensing another's "vibes" and those "gut" feelings we occasionally have just before we do the right things. Teachers are learning that a child's fidgeting and squirming are often an ally in disguise. Those who study the kinesthetic know that the body gets restless when it knows something the mind does not. Acknowledging both mind and body usually restores the harmony.

How this works is familiar to us all. Remember those times when you felt tense and apprehensive before entering a meeting or some social event? The mind had decided to go but the body sensed it was the wrong thing to do. Children in school also seem to know when they aren't going anywhere; their minds dutifully try to keep going yet their bodies are heading for the hills. Teachers who recognize this dissonance often are rewarded by stopping the lesson and asking the students to rise and express the concepts through movement.

There are dozens if not scores of effective therapeutic approaches for reuniting mind and body. Using the kinesthetic to quickly restore order is fine, but using it as standard daily practice in instruction and parenting is far more effective. Consider the following episode.

Once near dinner time our three-year-old son toddled up to me and laboriously climbed into a straight-backed dining room chair. He clambered about and established precarious postures, even tipping the chair to the edge of its balance point on several occasions. All the while, he kept uttering, "Daddy. . .daddydaddydaddydaddy," as he searched for some unknown way to ask straight out what he was obviously avoiding. My first reaction was to demand that he sit still and not abuse the furniture. But his antics contained their own fascination and I watched with growing enchantment. Eventually he sat upright and asked with great directness, "Daddy, can I have a popsicle?"

It was too close to dinner to have a popsicle and his mind knew that. However, his body (and its cravings) did not quite know it. He was hungry yet knew how inappropriate his request was. The gyrations and contortions on the chair were a kinesthetic exercise in gaining courage to convey his hazardous request. The mind-body connection is a two-way street. The mind can teach the body and the body can teach the mind. We need more than technologies of physical repression if we are to honor our evolutionary design.

Outward Bound and adventure programs have capitalized on the realization this this process operates both ways. Intense kinesthetic involvement while the mind is exploring new ideas and values insures a more holistic integration of mind and body. In parenting and teaching, the kinesthetic can be more realistically invited into pragmatic action. In Fort Myers, Florida, elementary school children under the guidance of Tom Walters and Bill Hammond were invited to use movement and invent dances that expressed the concepts in their curriculum. Subtraction, addition, sentence diagramming, parts of speech, the laws of gravity and democracy all became content for kinesthetic expression. The children showed remarkable improvements both on the standardized tests and the tests made by teachers.

The kinesthetic goes beyond the standard and socially-accepted forms of body movement. Dance and organized sports are the two most accepted options. Both stress the performance of established movement patterns and do not ordinarily allow for invention and innovation until expertise has been achieved. Children need to experience improvisation as well as conformity in the kinesthetic. They need to sense their own mind-body balance in life situations.

In his consciousness-transforming book, *The Primal Mind*, Jamake Highwater demonstrates that preliterate cultures have used the kinesthetic to encode history, philosophy, psychology and ethical laws. European settlers and missionaries interpreted such ritual movements or "dances" as expressions of pagan religion. European dance had evolved to repetitive, ritualistic, rule-bound forms indulged in primarily for entertainment. History, philosophy and the like were left to words and printing presses. Dance itself suffered once it moved out of tradition. Religious zealots saw non-traditional dances as the embodiment of evil. Translating human experience into symbolic codes and words facilitates reading but it also precludes subsequent diversity in modality experiences.

It is little wonder that primal people show traditions lasting thousands of years—they have re-experienced their traditions with each visual, kinesthetic and auditory recreation. Yet these same traditions wither as literacy blooms, as experience is translated into the coded symbolic processes of the mind alone. Rather than experiencing its vital synthesis, they reduce full sensory-intellectuality to fit the narrower logic of the codes.

Our current practices pertaining to kinesthetic wisdom at home and at school are limited. The primary concern of hundreds of parents I have interviewed and spoken with was their children's physical safety. They don't want their children to get hurt so they restrict kinesthetic risks. Parents often overdress children so the body doesn't experience normal temperature differences—they keep children from running, jumping and climbing to explore body use. That penchant for physical safety shifts at school to a concern for control. The rules for lining up, sitting straight, sitting still and facing forward are augmented by physical education activities where organized games and predefined experiences restrict body use.

Fortunately, emerging trends in physical education are beginning to stress kinesthetic wisdom. In some schools, competitive body contact sports are de-emphasized and more time is spent on physical education without team- or game-based emphases. These kinesthetic approaches provide a series of lifelong skills students can do alone, without the support of an organized team. Among these are downhill and cross-country skiing, snorkeling, scuba diving, backpacking and the most well-known, recreational running.

In experiences such as these, children have time to listen to their bodies and their minds. In America the sports of solitude are the fastest-growing form of entertainment and physical involvement. We seem to know it is time to again honor our design. People are carving out time to relate to the larger systems of the natural world in the ways that the primal people have done for centuries. We are learning again how to involve our bodies with nature in ways that first quiet and teach the mind. The spirituality so common to solitude is being restored. Children are being allowed to discover again that the world is basically a benevolent place and that they are part of it. The earth is the first teacher.

We must reinstate the notion that the body is an instrument of exploration and counter the idea that its primary use is for competition and combat.

There is an impressive data base emerging from the field of holistic health. It suggests that mind-body coordination and unity are central to health. What this means is that the two-thousand-year-old tradition of classical medicine that holds the healer and the healed as separate entities is simply wrong. We each must take an active role in our own healing, and the full responsibility for that healing is ours, not the doctor's. Even more significantly, we must take responsibility, to a large degree, for our health. This responsibility has at its core the premise of mind-body unity. The mind and body unite in healing and in teaching. Teaching thus becomes a healing profession.

Parenting must begin to slip its manacled mind-set about the body. We must relax the rigid perception that every time children use their bodies, they will be injured. We must reinstate the notion that the body is an instrument of exploration and experience. Children must be assured more access to natural settings and once there allowed more freedom to explore. Cleanliness and starched clothing can never gain more status than learning to walk on slippery mud, sliding on snow mounds and climbing the friendly branches of a sprawling tree. I am beginning to believe that parents remember the child's first step more because they recognize it as an acquisition of freedom—freedom that must be controlled. Somehow we have to learn to restore mind-body unity in the days past the child's first steps.

We are inheritors of a cultural perspective that has as a priority the repression and control of the body. Kinesthetic wisdom is being re-born into our cultural and philosophical milieu. We are finding out that we need our bodies to be able to more fully experience life in good health. Many are exploring specific approaches on their own. Others are finding guidance in the arts of dance and movement. Still others are seeking pathways in the martial arts. And others are returning to natural systems for the wisdom of eons past. In all these explorations, the body will no longer remain as an absent factor in its quest for unity with the mind. We are at a threshold of a more complete and basic kind of freedom and wellbeing.

Auditory

My first real awareness of the role of auditory function in the brain-mind system came one spring afternoon in Benjamin Franklin High School in Harlem. The teacher was setting up an exam, which involved passing out papers, giving instructions and maintaining demeanor. One black student was tapping his pencil on the desk in a complex and rhythmic cadence. He was oblivious to the others in the room. Playing to his own inner drummer, he seemed to be disturbing no one except the teacher, once she'd noticed him. Her reaction amused me, since for a full five minutes she had been distracted by other chores and had not reacted. Now she had a mission. She marched directly to his desk.

Although the student was "bugging" the teacher, he clearly was not intentionally doing so. He showed none of the facial and body cues that an intentional delinquent would have shown. He was simply playing "music" to her droning words. She didn't appreciate it and asked him to stop. At first he seemed not to know what she was talking about. He looked puzzled. "The pencil," she said. "Stop tapping that pencil." His eyes cast down and he was genuinely embarrassed.

As the test began, the teacher stood and then walked slowly about the room. She hadn't yet noticed that the drumming had resumed. It was softer now, as the student did it on the test booklet. When I was sure she was about to notice, I approached her and, in polite stage whispers, began a conversation about the class and the test they were taking. My distraction worked for a while but, as the students turned the test pages, resulting in fewer pages to dampen the sound, the drumming again became noticeable. With a darting movement, the teacher slashed toward the student and in words I could not hear made it clear that he was to stop the tapping.

His embarrassment was now complete. It was almost impossible for him to hide it. Yet I was convinced that his tapping had been reflexive and not at all malicious. Occasionally throughout the rest of the test the student would tap his rhythm on his teeth or hand. But nearly every time, a hard look from the teacher made him stop.

If you live in silence, you discover that there are lots of sounds in silence.
Elise Boulding

Several days later when the test was returned to the students, I revisited the classroom. I positioned myself by the student who had been drumming his way through the test. He was at it again. The tapping rhythm was identical to that of the day of the test. This day, however, the drumming seemed not to annoy the teacher. The discussion of the results and the mood of excitement created enough background noise to drown it out.

I watched him carefully. The music certainly was not random, nor did it seem to be drawn from other sources. It was original—and then it became clear to me. *The student was creating music, on the spot, to conform to the very words that were on each line of the test.* Suddenly the tapping stopped. I looked up to see if the teacher had spotted our grammatical musician, but she had not. He had stopped tapping at the very point he was told to stop during the original test.

As I looked at his paper it showed that he had missed only one answer to the point where the music stopped. But after that he missed fully two-thirds of the questions. Later, I asked him if I could talk with him. He agreed after he was sure I was not going to reprimand him.

Gently I drew out his version of the "music." He had always had trouble with reading. The pain caused by this in school led his mother to take action at home by showing him he could "read." She taught him to read sounds and then at a later time she taught him to read music. She played both the organ and the piano in their church and used these skills to help her son. It turned out that he was able to translate his skill with sound and music into a vital ally in the reading process. The only problem was creating acceptance in the schools. Teachers saw him as disruptive and cut off his most effective way to succeed in the world of book wisdom.

With the help of his mother, this young man had discovered a principle that many modern audiologists and neuroscientists are just beginning to apply. The brain-mind system creates order in the world through patterned sound and rhythm. For some, the whole basis for perception is linked to an intricate web of tonality, meter, rhythm and harmony. These same qualities are the heartblood of music, yet are broader than music.

Each culture has created the ritual expressions of some of its experience through patterned sound. We call this ritual expression "music." However, the modality which synthesizes these experiences within the brain-mind-body is its own unique form of wisdom—it is far *more* than music. Long before children develop speech, they form magnificent webs of perception and conception from what adults call "meaningless sound."

Sound is most probably the first of the senses other than touch experienced by the unborn child. The whooshing, gurgling sounds of the mother's circulatory and digestive systems are a child's first symphony. Locked in the oceanic realm of the amnion, these tiny humans are bathed in the world of the cetaceans—the whales and dolphins. The infant learns to structure the world by auditory input. Some months after conception, the brain begins to form the visual systems in both itself and the body. At this time, the dream-state sleep begins. But what is it that the infant dreams about? Whatever their content, dreams are drawn from the world of sound imbedded in the surrounding fluid world.

The mother's conversations also provide input. By talking to others, mothers create the sounds of their own speech and the children experience those as well. Too often we think of the auditory as accessed only through the ears. Remember that these early sounds are full body *vibrations*. Perhaps they can best be described as *seismic*. Many have ignored this aspect of the auditory until they see their children flock to rock music concerts to *feel* the music as well as hear it. Children feel the music of the womb. Some researchers have suggested that the interchanges between mothers and other people establish the music of the child's native language. There is some evidence that children who are taken from mothers at birth and raised in other cultures never get the rhythm of the new language as effectively as do native-born children. Sound in utero is not forgotten when speech is acquired.

Sound and vibratory experience along with the kinesthetic domain of touch, therefore, represent the earliest realms in which the unborn child acquires meaning. For us to ignore the possibilities of their intrinsic wisdom in parenting and teaching is tragic. Obviously, the Beethovens and Mozarts of history used their auditory graces to great credit. Providing for children greater access to these forms of wisdom is up to each parent and teacher.

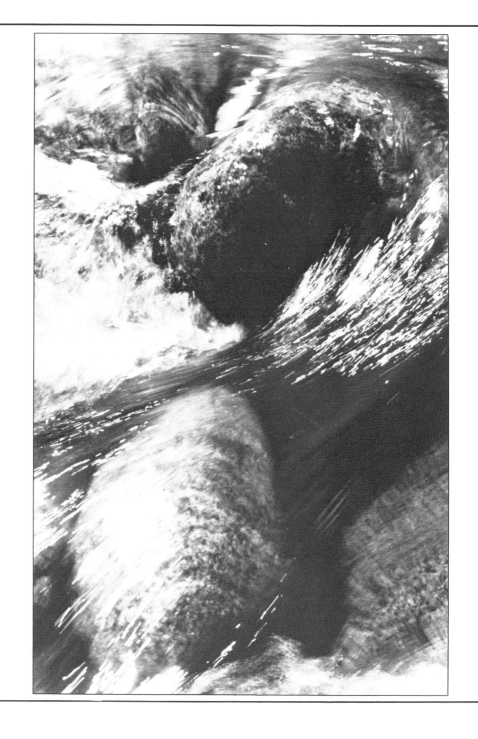

Synergic

As much as anyone else, Buckminster Fuller popularized and expanded the meaning of the word "synergy." Synergy is, in and of itself, mystical yet is reflected in every instant of existence. The world works synergetically. Synergy is expressed by the simultaneous interacting presence of several systems. The effect of synergy is to have the final expression of the interaction be greater than the accountable sum of the parts. Synergy produces greater results than knowledge can account for. 2 + 2 = 5 is synergy. When Elizabeth Barrett Browning wrote, "How do I love thee . . . let me but count the ways," the counting could have gone on to infinity.

As an idea, synergy contradicts our inherited Newtonian perceptions of mind and nature. For centuries, humans sliced the world into internally-consistent perspectives, treating each as distinct and separate. Science furthered this movement, providing the means by which the world could be understood via fragmentation.

What seemed beyond our comprehension for centuries was how the mind could change the rules of its own use. When we give up the rules for exclusivity, inclusivity results. We studied the brain in exclusive ways, ways guided by fragmentation. A veritable revolution took place when we shifted to a holistic and inclusive perspective.

The revolution in the neurosciences was accompanied by a revolution in physics and biology. It seems as though once the mind began to view itself differently, it began to see the world differently. The surgically-reductive qualities of mind now seem destined to give way to a more pervasive healing kind of unity—a synergic unity. We have begun to rediscover how to think whole.

In the synergic mode the mind creates a rich and surprisingly new synthesis of all the modalities—Symbolic-Abstract, Visual, Kinesthetic and Auditory. Synergic knowing gives birth to insight, outsight, intuition and creativity. In this mode, the mind almost confounds itself with its abilities.

The Synergic mode includes knowledge of self, relationships with others, and connections with natural systems. Those of us who are exploring synergy immerse in the bond between mind and nature. Gregory Bateson wrote intensely about this bond in his final book, *Mind and Nature: A Necessary Unity*, in which he analyzed the biological tenets relating natural systems, evolution and mind. My books *The Metaphoric Mind* and *Mind of Our Mother* explore similar contexts.

Many authors have explored the workings of the Synergic modality via creativity. Brewster Ghiselin, W. J. J. Gordon, Paul Torrance and dozens of others, including myself, have tried with varying degrees of frustration. Synergy by definition defies precise analysis. Authors such as Donald Perkins in his book, *Mind's Best Work*, have explored creativity non-synergically and have emerged somewhat disappointed and disappointing. Perkins ignores the oceans of possibility and sails into an embayment of reductive analysis in search of creativity—a voyage devoid of success. Robert Weisberg follows much the same course in his book, *Creativity.*

Creativity is an expression of the Synergic modality. More will be said about creativity later, but for now let us rest on Erich Jantsch's claim that creativity is evolution unfolding. Synergy describes creation. Details are tantalizingly absent from the creative process.

Einstein once said, "The most beautiful and profound emotion that one can experience is the sense of the mystical . . . it is the dower of all true science." Certainly, he possessed a synergic mind; yet was his gift so unique? Perhaps we, too, may nurture mystical ways of knowing. Einstein's genius arose from the convergence of an extraordinary brain and a courageous mind. He had the courage to be open and the vision to be whole. Like Einstein, we must develop the vision to establish and the courage to maintain openness and wholeness.

Understanding is not static knowledge, but itself an evolutionary process.
Erich Jantsch

Teachers and parents are unhealthily biased toward instant results. They seek to understand all the details of a child's answers and solutions, potentially damaging the Synergic modality. When I encourage a child to explore the diversity of the learning modalities and to harvest them synergically, I am prepared to *not* understand. I accept the child's spontaneity of solution and the possible long-term incubation and gestation of ideas. The Synergic modality is the modality of whole-brainedness and of brain-mind-body unity.

In synergic function we see in children a blending of excitement with a firm sense of peace. We sense that they *know* something—without having learned it. They speak confidently—with a conviction that comes from within and is unrelated to approval from outside sources. They appear to be privy to some coalescing form of unity.

I was once out driving with our four-year-old son, running errands in a town near our home. My mind was filled with where we were going and what we had to do. Stician was amusing himself in the back seat. Suddenly I became aware that he was speaking stridently—loudly issuing a proclamation of some sort. I missed the first few lines so I asked him to repeat them. He did so without hesitation and repeated exactly what he had said. The message startled me with its poignance and profundity. I stopped the car and took the following notes:

> It's a place. . .a master place inside us that belongs to everyone. No! Everything! It's the place that makes all the trees and all the mountains and all the people one thing. It makes me want to say what I know so there will be peace and all things will stop dying. All the things that are, are really all one thing. I know this and I say it.

The bustle of the classroom and home frequently masks the moments when such synergy occurs. Parents' and teachers' attentions are divided, and they let recognition of these near-holy events slip into the wastelands of fragmented life. Children often do not know what just happened to them and their uncertainty overrides the confidence they momentarily felt.

Each time I have had the privilege to witness such synergy, I have done so from what can be called "center." I have been at peace within my own brain-mind-body. From such a synergic condition I was swept into the event. Many teachers and parents have also realized that they noticed their children's most profound "learnings" when they, the adults, were calm and relaxed.

Perhaps synergy and centeredness are symbiotic. They nurture and sustain each other. They are part of the same ecology of mind. The apparently disproportionate space I devote to centering in *OPENMIND/WHOLEMIND* (Part V) may betray the value I place in this art. One intriguing consequence of the premise of centering and centeredness is that every point within an infinite universe is its center. Therefore as I learn to center, I learn to better honor my fit in the universe. I, you and everything else are wedded in concept and context to each other. As I honor my own center, I must honor yours, each child's and the gaseous nebulae in the constellation of Cygnus. Even if the universe should turn out to be finite the same would hold true. The difference is that we would simply have to ask our mind to *behave as though it were all infinite!* From such a premise, we are more susceptible to the whispers as well as the shouts in the journeys through the immensity of our mindscapes.

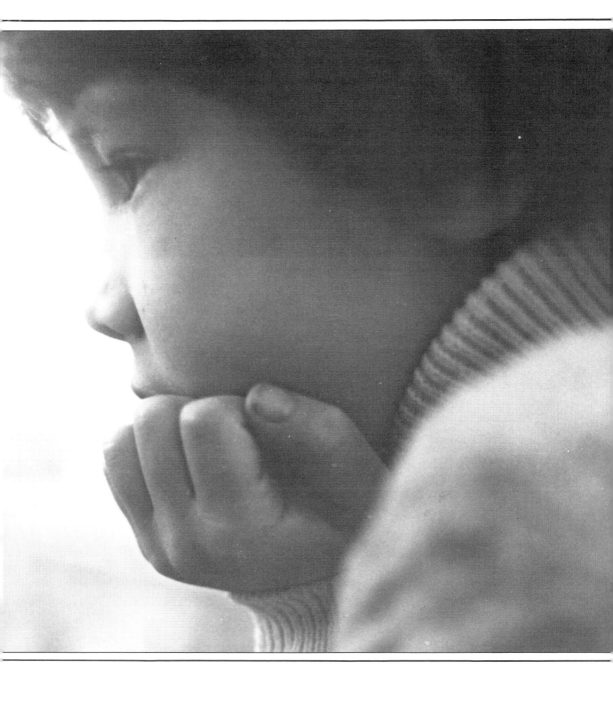

Intelligences

In his 1982 book, *Frames of Mind: A Theory of Multiple Intelligences*, Howard Gardner describes seven distinct forms of intelligence. Gardner defines intelligence as the capacity to do something useful in society. My list of modalities is similar to Gardner's list of multiple intelligences. See the table below.

Samples		Gardner
Symbolic-Abstract	———	Verbal-Linguistic Mathematical-Logical
Visual-Spatial	———	Spatial
Kinesthetic	———	Bodily Kinesthetic
Auditory	———	Musical
Synergic	———	Personal
Personal		Interpersonal
Natural		Intrapersonal

In the early 1960s, Gardner was a graduate student of Jerome Bruner at Harvard University's Center for Cognitive Studies. At that time, I worked with Bruner on the National Science Foundation-funded projects, "Elementary Science Study" and "Man: A Course of Study." Bruner thus was a mentor to both Gardner and myself.

Gardner states that the Mathematical-Logical and Linguistic forms of intelligence are the most favored in our society. These correlate with the modality I term Symbolic-Abstract—the use of coded symbols. My Visual and Gardner's Spatial are a direct match. Auditory and Musical represents another match, but I am convinced that auditory wisdom covers a larger context than music. I clarified this in part—with the example of a student needing rhythmic sound to perform on tests. Finally, there is a correspondence between my Kinesthetic modality and his Bodily-Kinesthetic intelligence.

My experience with R. Buckminster Fuller convinced me that both human systems *and* nature must be accounted for and require a synergic approach. Gardner's last intelligence is Personal which he subdivides into Intra-personal and Inter-personal—knowing one's self and knowing how to relate to others. I accept these distinctions but add a third which includes input-output and empathy with *nature*—natural systems. Empathy used in reference to nature is unconventional. However, I am convinced that such an empathy is central to our species having survived. Parenting and teaching can rekindle that empathy and nurture it for future survival.

Another vibrant voice in the arena of multiple intelligences is that of Robert Sternberg at Yale University. While his views offer a departure from the modality-intelligence link, Sternberg speaks well to the Synergic modality. He describes three qualities of intelligence that are cast across the modalities in a way that embodies synthesis. He seems less interested in the design of the brain-mind system than in the way people integrate their capabilities into a style of doing useful things in society.

The first of Sternberg's intelligences is called *Contextual*. Persons exhibiting this kind of intelligence are highly adaptable. They selectively shape environments related to their life. They make the most of what they have, optimizing *any* modality-intelligence to best suit their experience.

Sternberg's second intelligence is called *Experiential*. In this form the learner is capable of engaging in novel experience and making sense of it. This form of intelligence seems more responsive than adaptive. Persons with this intelligence are adept with *new* rather than *old* knowledge. Moreover, people with this kind of intelligence can quickly and automatically convert what they experience into a useful form. In a sense, they see the big picture and behave accordingly.

The third form of intelligence is *Componential*. These people recognize the patterns of interrelatedness in the component parts of thinking, learning and knowing. This is the kind of intelligence that has been tested most fully. Planning, performance and acquisition of knowledge are central to this kind of intelligence.

In many ways Gardner's and Sternberg's views of intelligence are compatible. Using Gardner's definition, "the capacity to do something useful in the society in which you live," it seems clear that intelligence is multifaceted, multisensory and multidimensional. Sternberg offers us a more analytic view of the applications of input, output and the processing that goes on in between. Both are useful and illuminating. They both tell us that much is going on while we engage our brain-mind systems.

What I feel is most productive is that Gardner honors the variety of ways humans have been designed to be intelligent or "useful" in their society. Sternberg points out the various ways people synthesize their design in order to be useful. Suffice it to say that diversity is the key factor.

Intelligences are expressions of how our learning modalities are made useful in society. Western society has tended to emphasize the forms of intelligence that are represented through abstract codes. It is our ability to use these codes and reason within their rules that establishes our "intelligence quotient" or I.Q.

Schools, through teachers, manage children in the pursuit of intelligence—the acquisition of usefulness. Within the two fundamental settings—home and school—children gain confidence in both their design and their usefulness. With parents, children can learn to honor their modalities through experiences aimed at building self esteem, self image, confidence and skill. Parents can nurture an inherent respect and acceptance for all the modalities, not just the Symbolic-Abstract. Teachers can nurture the growth of the learning modalities and help children connect skills with the development of a variety of intelligences. Schools that overemphasize the Mathematical-Logical and Linguistic intelligences (the basics!) deny children the experience of developing as whole human beings with diverse talents.

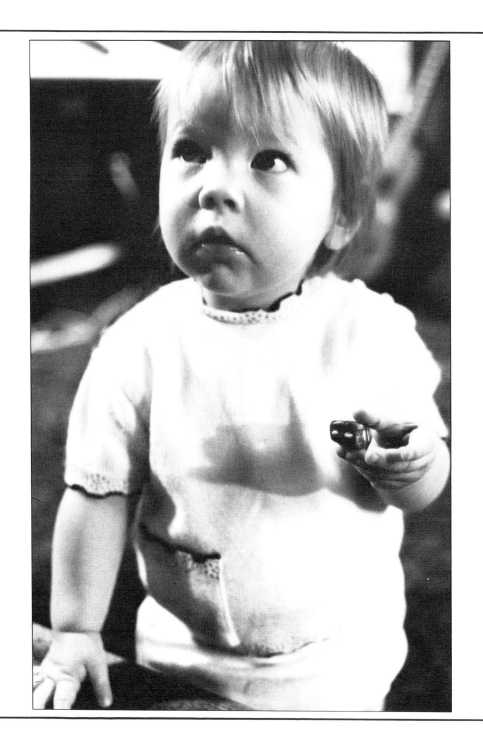

Learning Styles

Learning styles are the ways we prefer to process experience and information. They are habits, reflecting how we treat the experience that we gain through the modalities. But learning styles are different from modalities. *How* we prefer to learn is a choice. For instance, whether we prefer active experimentation or reflective observation does not depend on which modality we use. Theoretically, a person can have both a preferred learning style as well as a preferred modality, or one can stick to the same learning style to process sensory experience from all modalities. Or, one can develop flexibility and employ each of the learning styles and each of the modalities at will.

Although many pioneered in the field of learning styles, few have been more comprehensive than Bernice McCarthy. Her work represents an approach that is most consistent with what we know about the brain-mind system. I appreciate her understanding and commitment to the contemporary neurosciences. Moreover, she clearly understands the differences between learning modalities, learning styles and ecological factors in the learning process.

147

McCarthy began by recognizing the similarity among the basic models of a dozen researchers in the field. All seemed influenced by the original work of C. G. Jung. David Kolb was foremost in having established a research base that illuminated McCarthy's path. Although aware of variations among the different models, McCarthy also recognized their similarities. Her primary contribution was to synthesize the lot, characterizing processing tendencies or preferences that guide learning.

She gleaned from this diverse search four preferences or habits in processing information, shown below:

CONCRETE EXPERIENCE

ACTIVE EXPERIMENTATION — REFLECTIVE OBSERVATION

ABSTRACT CONCEPTUALIZATION

The vertical axis pairs CONCRETE EXPERIENCE and ABSTRACT EXPERIENCE.

Learners preferring *Concrete Experience* are those who have strong qualities of sensing and feeling. They have richly sensual experiences leavened with emotion and a central concern for feelings. Learners at the opposite end of this vertical axis prefer *Abstract Concepts* and objectivity. These learners use other modalities dominantly to collect and process information to form concepts that are basically free of emotion and feeling.

The horizontal axis pairs ACTIVE EXPERIMENTATION and REFLECTIVE OBSERVATION.

Those preferring *Active Experimentation* are the doers. They get involved at once via the kinesthetic and other sensory modalities. Their chosen route is one that requires action and they reflexively initiate it. The other end of the axis represents learners who prefer to watch and reflect. Theirs is the dimension of *Reflective Observation*. For these learners, the act of learning is one of contemplation and quiet watching.

The vertical axis describes a learner's preferences in terms of intent and outcome. The concrete learner establishes a highly subjective and personal quality to the learning; the abstract shows a marked preference for the objective. The vertical axis may well represent a learner's commitment to the ultimate outcome of a learning experience. The concrete learner will seek personal meaning while the abstract learner seeks an objective "truth."

The horizontal axis describes behavior. Its descriptors characterize how one goes about learning. Learners at one extreme are action-oriented (*Active Experimentation*) while those at the other are more passive (*Reflective Observation*).

Learners are always a combination of both axes. That is, each person has habits of intent and of behavior. Whenever learning takes place, a purpose or intent (the vertical axis) and an action or behavior (the horizontal axis) are present.

This means that we combine the various descriptors to establish one's preferred style of learning. This is precisely how McCarthy arrived at the *4-MAT System*. The following diagram illustrates the relationships between the axis descriptors and the *4-MAT* quadrants.

4MAT is a registered trademark of Excel Incorporated and Bernice McCarthy.

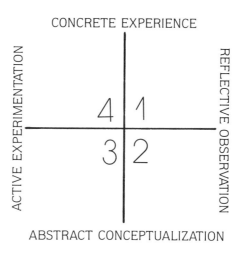

The four learning styles indicated in the diagram are combinations of the intent and behavior involved in the learning experience. Each quadrant represents two qualities. For example, Quadrant 1 learners are committed to CONCRETE EXPERIENCE and REFLECTIVE OBSERVATION. Quadrant 3 learners are guided by an intent on ABSTRACT CONCEP-TUALIZATION and their behavior is reflected in direct action via ACTIVE EXPERIMENTATION.

The importance in all this is certainly not in either classifying or labeling. McCarthy's format systematically frames an expression of differences in learning habits and preferences. It also guides teachers and parents to methods that offer each learner a chance for success. The Quadrant 1 learner has different requirements from the Quadrant 3 learner. The former wants concrete experience and quiet for reflection and the latter wants action and abstraction.

Even more important is the fact that the adult (teacher and/or parent) also has a learning style. Research is replete with evidence showing that teachers teach to their own style or to the style the school demands via their evaluation policies (typically Quadrant 2). What this means is that, if I am your teacher, I will teach from my own style or the school's preferred style, not necessarily from yours.

McCarthy's system is a framework for identifying learning styles, and—even more important—a process for systematically allowing children to explore options in learning. This last point is precisely why I have included this discussion of learning styles. If a teacher or parent can systematically provide learning modality and learning style options, the child is more likely to experience whole-minded learning. The child is more apt to excel in all areas, to have a positive self image and to experience feelings of success and accomplishment.

Learning Styles: General Characteristics

Quadrant 1 Learners

Preference for CONCRETE EXPERIENCE and REFLECTIVE OBSERVATION

Personal meaning is of primary importance to Quadrant 1 learners. They must gain some personal worth from instruction and may resist starting until they are satisfied that meaning will be there. They prefer to listen and then conversationally discuss ideas. Group discussion, particularly small group discussions which nurture conversation, is their favorite classroom method. They are very interested in people and believe strongly in their own experience. They model after people they respect. They are innovative in the realm of ideas that relate to people. They seek to establish unity and agreement among all members of a group. Discord and lack of consensus leave them uneasy and uncomfortable.

As children their favorite activities might be birthday parties, school, sunday school and camp. Some, inclined toward more solitude, might like hiking and playing alone. Sometimes Quadrant 1 children might seek time with quiet thoughtful adults. As adults their favorite psychology books might include Victor Frankel's *Man's Search for Meaning* and Carl Rogers' *On Becoming a Person.* They are drawn toward humanistic psychology. Sentimentalism and passionate social concerns might guide their daily perception. Their friends are cared for and nurtured.

Healthy Quadrant 1 learners are empathic, considerate and cooperative. Interpersonal involvement is a product of the joy of being together and emphasizes the benefits of cooperation.

Pathological Quadrant 1 learners are manipulative and hold extremely high expectations of others. Unhealthy Quadrant 1 people are imprisoned in their own ego demands. They require constant attention to their well being and enforce dependency in relationships.

Quadrant 2 Learners

Preference for REFLECTIVE OBSERVATION and ABSTRACT CONCEPTUALIZATION

Learners in this quadrant are the keepers of the truth. They require facts, accuracy and orderliness. They are comforted by rules and they form reality from them. They are attentive to experts but are less interested in people in general. However, if they believe in a person's scholarship or authority they may admire them enthusiastically and establish them as role models. These learners are driven toward "right" answers and their loyalty to what is right is quite strong. When they need to make decisions, their first cry is for facts. They believe in rationality and logic as primary virtues.

They are the happiest when they are operating in a field of endeavor that is well defined, the expectations are explicit and attainable. As children they might indulge for hours in the instruction manuals that come with toys. They might become anguished if parts turn out to be missing or if there are several pieces left over. Adult entertainment for them might be crossword puzzles and listening to classical music for its discipline and form. They are drawn toward science, mathematics, accounting and careers marked by high precision and accuracy. If they were interested in psychology as adults, their favorite books would be authoritative and scholarly. B. F. Skinner's *Behavioral Psychology* might be an example.

As children they might like hopscotch, 4-square and other games with definite rules and boundaries. In school, they are grade-conscious and pursue the things that produce the "right" answer.

Healthy Quadrant 2 learners are marvels of detail and accuracy. They prize form and procedures in expression and can be depended on to be thorough and precise. When they offer something, you can be sure that it has been researched and checked for accuracy. They often require more time than seems necessary, but this is only to check and countercheck the accuracy of their work.

Pathological 2s are marked by a compulsion to be complete. They are never satisfied that enough data are available and often will obstruct progress with their insatiable need for more information. Often the unhealthy demand for precision will make the Quadrant 2 learner (parent or teacher) a closed-system totalitarian of order and rules. Of all the *4-MAT System* learners, the 2s are the most susceptible to being closed. This inclination makes sense if we remember that the weight of history and tradition has established the precedents which they can easily see as "right."

Quadrant 3 Learners

Preference for ACTIVE EXPERIMENTATION and ABSTRACT CONCEPTUALIZATION

Almost before one can blink an eye these learners are engaged in action. Matching their compulsion to act is the requirement that what they learn be useful and applicable. Their primary attraction to the arena of abstract conceptualization is that it provides theories to be actively tested. They detest the disclosure of answers before they have had enough time to explore possible solutions. They are practical and want to learn things they can use in everyday life. They cherish "facts," which are seen as the raw material for action.

As children they are the ones who don't discover until Easter that instructions were included in the gifts they received at Christmas. They are always out of their seats at the moment the bell rings. Their favorite bumper sticker or tee shirt reads "READY-FIRE-AIM." Teachers and parents find these children to be uncooperative in that they are unable to "wait for instructions." They are also reluctant to defer action and rewards. To "save up" money, credits or rewards seems absurd to them. The only way deferment can make sense to them is if *the act of deferment can be made into the action they are seeking*.

As adults they are born interventionists. They are seen as no-nonsense types that want to get the job done. Often they become so intent on the action they tend to become insensitive to those around them. If they are interested in psychology it would be a laboratory focus and a "how to do it manual," perhaps one of Wayne Dyer's books.

Healthy 3s get things done. They can be depended upon to meet deadlines and produce high quality work. Since they are so action-oriented, their skills often show great maturity. As soon as they feel confident in your trust, they are quick to recognize the need for action before others do and will often save the day. They never forget to feed the hamster and check the fish tank.

Pathological Quadrant 3 learners are compulsive meddlers. They take action reflexively and tend to snarl things up—they over-act on events. If they have an idea, they might immediately attempt to test it without regard for the consequences. An unhealthy 3 might read about an abstract technique, take it home, to school or the office and apply it wholesale without regard for the needs of others involved.

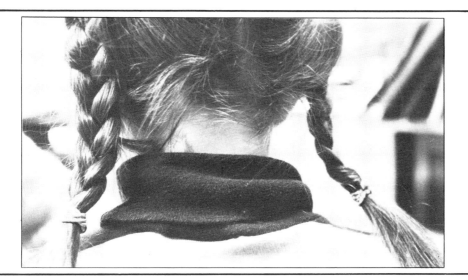

Quadrant 4 Learners

Preferences for CONCRETE EXPERIENCE and ACTIVE EXPERIMENTATION

These are self-discovery learners. They have a strong need to experience freedom in their learning and have a tendency to transform whatever it is they attempt. They are at home with making decisions since they are so flexible. A bad decision will only be a temporary setback. They are highly intuitive and often come to valid conclusions that are not logically justified. Quadrant 4 learners are born risk takers and for them failure is positive feedback. They are often seen as inconsiderate of others. This is not intentional as they are frequently lost in a task and will seem to abandon common courtesies. Once reminded of the breach of consideration they tend to apologize and get back on task.

As children, Quadrant 4 learners are highly inventive and self-entertaining. It seems their only encounter with teachers and parents is when they are seeking more tools or advice on a self-designated task. For them any assignment is appropriate since they will do with it what they want anyway. Their life pattern is a search for possibility and change. Should their interests turn to psychology they would indulge in Abraham Maslow's *The Farther Reaches of Human Nature*.

The healthy learners in Quadrant 4 are self-reliant and self-directing. They respect form and procedure but recognize the need for it out of their own inquiry. Once it is recognized, they will discipline themselves and acquire whatever skills they need for accomplishing their purposes.

Pathological 4s are nearly always overcommitted and fragmented. They never seem to develop the discipline to finish one task before they attempt another. This is different from being able to do several things at once. Being fragmented means they know at the outset they will never finish the commitment but can't resist the novelty of beginning. For them newness is so seductive they are drawn in regardless of the consequences. The result is that they seldom develop the skills or acquire the information to complete work with integrity.

Honoring and Extending Learning Styles

School administrators have looked at research related to learning styles to improve students' school performance. This effort has had some successes: grades and test results have risen in places where learning style approaches have been used.

With their attention riveted on improvement in schoolwork, many school administrators have chosen to determine the teachers' learning and teaching style and then match students accordingly. Such compatibility was supposed to produce more rapid positive results in the students' performance. When matched with a compatible student, the teacher performs in a mode favored by the student. Disturbingly, however, both teacher and student are systematically deprived of experience and growth in other learning styles. This kind of matching can produce short-term gains in performance but also long-term deficits. It breeds specialization. This practice is a classic example of the emphasis on *schoolwork* over *lifework*.

Recent research confirms this. Matching teachers and students by learning styles produces the poorest results in overall academic achievement. The same research shows that the best results come when administrators help teachers understand the consequences of the differing learning styles and then assign them students of all four styles. This creates intentional heterogeneity rather than homogeneity, a generalized environment rather than a specialized one.

Specialization of the sort cited above is against the fabric of *OPEN-MIND/WHOLEMIND*. Here, we are endeavoring to increase *flexibility and fluency* in thought. Honoring and developing this flexibility and fluency of thought are perhaps the most vital ways we can address the uncertainty of the future. Remember that specialization produces the conditions for extinction. With this in mind, let us explore the tasks and assignments most compatible with each learning style. Although each assignment will appeal most strongly to those students with that learning style preference, it will enable students with other preferences to increase their repertoires.

Just a note: Research does indicate that the matching of teacher-learner styles is remarkably effective if the student is severely deprived of "normal" recourse. Severely handicapped children are benefitted from the role model of a matched teacher and gain confidence and self esteem from the experience. However, when adjustment is made, the exposure to the various other styles is necessary for further growth.

Diversity nurtures survival.
Specialization nurtures extinction.

QUADRANT 1 LEARNERS: High Concrete Experience and Reflective Observation

Want to know WHY in a personal way.

Sample Assignments:

Describe the event in the story that was most meaningful to you. Identify your favorite color, flower, animal or song and describe how they make you feel. Discuss the role of feelings with three other people of your choice. How would your life be different if a woman were president? Determine how math is important to your life. Paint a picture that illustrates your feelings right now. Go outside and map the campus so that the map shows how you feel in each place you map. Invent a "perfect" friend and describe how they dress, talk and treat you.

QUADRANT 2 LEARNERS: High Abstract Conceptualization and High Reflective Observation

Want to know WHAT to do and need for there to be a "right" answer.

Sample Assignments:

Alphabetize the names of the children in the class. Find the five misspelled words in this paragraph. Diagram these sentences. How many basketballs would this room hold? Find words that rhyme and list them. Discuss the five main reasons for the Civil War. Write a report about the life cycle of butterflies. Find out how many desks there are in this school. List the names and addresses of our state's Senators and Representatives.

QUADRANT 3 LEARNERS: High Abstract Conceptualization and High Active Experimentation

Want to know HOW and want to be able to DO it.

Sample Assignments:

Make a cage for the gerbils. Paint a sign for the bake sale. Interview three people you like and three you don't like. Determine where the garden should be. See if you can take this clock apart. Find the plans for an intercom system that will allow you to communicate with the students in the next room. Make a collage that shows how democracy works. Find the best place for the can opener and install it. Make a set of flash cards with ten nouns, ten verbs, and ten adjectives. Find out what we need to raise mice and get the materials.

QUADRANT 4 LEARNERS: High Concrete Experience and High Active Experimentation

Want to be left alone to DISCOVER things themselves; once they do, they ask, WHAT IF?

The concept is *fear*—provide me with your understanding of fear in three days. The answer is *blue*—what was the question? Create an advertisement for lessening world hunger. Write a story we should have read this year. Identify something your friends should know and teach it to them. Find out five uses for things in this room that are uses they were not designed for. Find something that needs to be done in the community and get it done.

Use the examples above to generate additional ideas of your own. Students in school and children at home can be invited into thoughtful action in countless ways. The earlier this process is started, the greater the chance for developing a balance in the ways children process experience. They can begin to see the mind as a servant to their explorations. When seeking meaning, facts, action or practical application, students can marshal the skills and competencies of all the quadrants.

Again the cry is for wholeness. A balance between ambiguity and specificity ensures wholeness in brain-mind function. The intentional use of the entire array of learning modalities ensures wholeness. So, too, does the comprehensive honoring of all the learning styles.

When we hear the old saw that we use only ten percent of our brains, we must counter it on two fronts. The first is that it is wrong neurophysiologically. We cannot *not* use our whole brain. But we may not *pay attention* to what our brains are doing. This brings us to the second issue about how much of our brain is working. We now know that how much of our brain-mind we pay attention to is a matter of choice. *If we choose to pay attention to a wider array of mind functions, all we need do is get on with it.* There is no physiological reason for the limitations we have contrived. The limitations are attitudinal.

Through the learning modalities, multiple intelligences and learning style models we can access our own brain-mind systems beyond the entrenchment of habits we acquired earlier. Simultaneously, we can assist children at home and in school to avoid such entrenchment. And we can celebrate the open, flexible possibilities our brain-mind-bodies are genetically endowed to explore. This brings us to creativity.

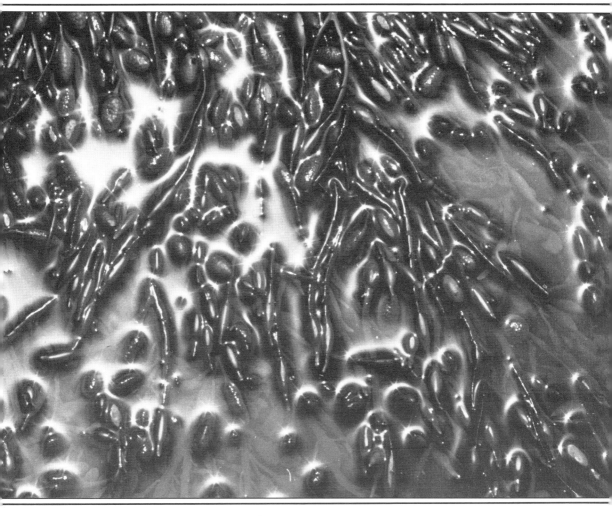

Creativity

Each of the ways of experiencing learning that we have explored has honored diversity. The modalities are aimed at extending the number of ways that we access and express experience in the world. The multiple intelligences are expressions of the many ways that cultures have found the modalities to be useful. Learning styles provide evidence for the variety that exists in how we process experience. All together there is little solace for those who wish to limit learning to a single modality, intelligence or style.

Yet our culture has established favorites. The Symbolic-Abstract modalities, Mathematical-Logical and Linguistic intelligences, and the Quadrant 2 learning style are clearly given priority. Those who are able, through their actions, to demonstrate strengths in several modalities, competence in a variety of intelligences and comfort in two or more learning styles are seen as unique. Yet this uniqueness is an accident of history rather than of design. *OPENMIND/WHOLEMIND* is dedicated to the proposition that all humans are created diverse—they are designed to be able to achieve competence and grace in a wide range of attributes of the brain-mind system.

When such diversity exists, the likelihood of creativity is heightened. Creativity—the C in M.I.S.C.--is a much-argued concept. About half those who study it are impressed with the mysticism that they see as the central characteristic of creativity. Others, even more adamant, are convinced that creativity is an extended form of rational-logical reasoning. Some say it is a gift and others maintain it can be taught. As was discussed in the section on Kubie and Freud, it is evident that some have even suggested it is a form of mental illness. Maslow and I each have maintained that it represents a high synthesis in mind work that inevitably results in peak experience and fulfillment.

Creativity may express itself in one's dealing with children, in making love, in carrying on a business, in formulating physical theory, in painting a picture.
Jerome Bruner

Although these arguments cannot be resolved to the satisfaction of all, it is fair to say that creativity is enhanced by diversity of experience, it can be taught and—once the act is complete—it can be explained. Thus the broadening of experiences by multimodality involvement, the recognition of wider usefulness through multiple intelligences and the application of the range of learning styles increase the likelihood of novelty in the solution of problems and the products of thought.

Creativity requires the modification of thought. It results in an outcome that is identifiably new or novel. The old must be transformed. Beyond that, there is a requirement of usefulness. This usefulness guarantees that whatever is created will live on in the mind of the creator. If what is created has usefulness beyond the mind of the person creating it, then public or social recognition may follow. Thus we must consider a public as well as a private side to creativity. When a child synthesizes his or her experience into a new (for the child) vision, creativity has been experienced. This is the personal or private form. If the vision brings newness to the culture then we are witnessing the public form of creativity.

There is a somewhat frightening aspect to creativity—it disturbs the status quo. Creativity is feared by those who passionately preserve things as they are. This is true whether we are considering a single brain-mind system or an entire society. The fear of creativity results in closedness. The individual hardens his or her defenses against change and the mind indulges in resisting the change necessary for creativity. The society does the same by entrenching in tradition and enforcing closedness.

In parenting and teaching we have the possibility to allow children to choose courage in the face of the tentative, to experience a wide array of options in mind use and to greet change and stability as compatible conditions. Change is necessary for creativity but so too is stability. Change drives the process and stability confirms it.

As a parent and teacher I must affirm the integrity of creativity:

Creativity is more than mere change.
Creativity includes accuracy and precision.
Creativity is possible in all modalities, intelligences and styles.
Creativity is both public and private.
Creativity results in useful and aesthetic expression.
Creativity begins in diversity and ends in specificity.
Creativity requires both openness and closedness.
Creativity is evolutionary.
Creativity is attitudinal.
Creativity is manifested in lifestyle.

A Summary Statement About M.I.S.C.

M.I.S.C. is a way of tracing and insuring diversity, success and competence. By intentionally creating settings where children are invited to demonstrate competence in less familiar ways, we can begin to prepare them for the unknown challenges of the future. Children would not exist in the present if they were not designed to cope with and be fulfilled by the future. It is our choice to invite them to realize the completeness of their design and guide them toward a responsible, self-regulating destiny.

EPISODES, REFLECTIONS AND EXPLORATIONS

PART V

Episodes, Reflections and Explorations

This section presents in-depth methods for honoring the various modalities in teaching and parenting. Episodes are short case histories. Reflections are commentaries from the perspectives of parenting and teaching. Explorations are one-line assignments that can extend or enrich a child's involvement in learning.

These approaches are starting points. Those who use multimodal explorations are quick to see new pathways that emerge as a result. The real thrill comes when the books lie closed and true inquiry begins. Even as you read these suggestions, remember that inquiry is born in the mind of the explorer, not in the mind of some external guide. By definition inquiry means the outcome or answer is unknown.

Parents and teachers both ask too many questions. Children are not comfortable with inquisition—they feel they are being put on trial. The result is that they hesitate to share their progress because disclosure leads to a string of new questions, high-pressure interrogation and forced verbalization.

Please note that questioning is absent or minimized in these episodes. This is the hardest part for most adults. My colleagues and I have discovered through research that adults use the interrogative about ninety percent of their time with children and teenagers. Children cannot giggle, whisper, sit in silence, close the bathroom door, run water in a sink, look in the refrigerator or even read without someone demanding, "What are you doing?"

At school it is even worse, since so much of instructional time is spent in interrogation. The so-called "inquiry" approaches that filtered into education during the 1960s and 70s are replete with non-ending strings of questions. Almost every act, for the six-and-a-half hours that most children spend each day in school, requires justification. They must tell *why* they wrote what they did, why they chose a particular topic, *why* they didn't do their homework, *what* they are doing at any moment and *how* they expect to improve. In professional settings we can establish the intensity of stress-inducing factors by the frequency of questions asked in discourse.

167

Questions in discourse are acts of aggression. They demand that something be disclosed that is not being disclosed. Readers may be surprised to learn that the languages of most of the primal societies (this includes nearly all Native Indian cultures) do not have an interrogative form. Most of these people did not ask questions until exposure to Europeans.

Adults spend nearly ninety percent of their time in the interrogative when they are around children—the questions are non-stop.

The alternative to questioning is disclosure by adults—disclosure in the declarative. Instead of saying, "What is that?" the more open response is, "I don't know what that is." The child is not tacitly forced to respond, but may choose to provide the information the adult does not possess. This approach also has the grace to convey to children that adults do not know everything.

One of the basic requirements of shifting from interrogation to disclosure—and this is of vital importance—is that *the disclosure must be honest*. Compulsive interrogators are clever at disguising questions as declarations. This is, at best, a form of deceit and has no place in the relationship between adult and child.

Make no mistake, there is a role for questions. They should be asked when an adult *does* want a child to defend his or her exploration. However, there is no defense for the ninety percent of the time currently devoted to questioning as the basis for adult-child discourse.

In terms of the Visual, Auditory and Kinesthetic modalities, students quickly learn that any expression in these modes is going to be questioned. This means that each time students explore in these modes, they begin to construct an elaborate defense of their actions. They know that the final act of any exploration will be reported in words or writing. This clearly diminishes the inherent fullness of these modalities. Children must experience an honoring from both teachers and parents of the Visual, Auditory and Kinesthetic modalities for the mindwork they engender. Art, music and dance, as well as the synergic combinations of these, are basic expressions of the human brain-mind design and deserve to be respected without defense. In addition, the more traditional Symbolic-Abstract modalities can be approached with more openness and flexibility.

None of the activities that follow involves single modalities. For example, it is impossible to isolate the visual and auditory while doing a kinesthetic activity. Each activity, however, is designed to enhance talents and capacities that are frequently neglected and overlooked. Whole humans have access to all of their modalities.

Episode 1 The Lost Galactic War

The scene was a classroom of third graders in an inner city school in Detroit. The teacher was white and enthusiastic and the students were hopeful. This was the first week of school. As soon as the children were settled, the teacher moved to a table filled with drawing paper, paints, brushes, crayons and colored pencils. With music in her voice she said, "I want you all to come to the table when I call your row. When you get here, I want you to choose some art supplies that you like and take them and one piece of paper to your desks."

All went well considering how enthusiastic third graders are about art. Art on the *first* day of school was heaven sent. I was close to a charming, bubbly little boy who knew that this was going to be his year. Already he had paper, four colored pencils and six crayons. Like the other children who were now in their seats, he squirmed with anticipation for the assignment. The teacher began, "I want you to draw or paint a picture that shows something happening. You can choose anything you want and you can draw for twenty minutes."

No more was needed. All the children dove into the assignment and work-ed in a silence that was broken only with murmurs of enjoyment. Occasionally children borrowed colors from each other and the art forms grew in detail and intensity. The boy closest to me had created an epic drawing of warfare in the future. It was replete with sleek spacecraft and domed cities. All was in chaos and factions were annihilating each other with great success. Some of the craft had plummeted to the planet and great smoketrails marked their course. Insignias were divided among the spaceships—the "good-guys" had starburst designs while the "evil-doers" sported cobras. The cobras were in trouble.

I was so engrossed that I hadn't noticed the teacher moving about the class, talking quietly with the children about their work. She slipped in beside my little artist and looked thoughtfully at his work. After a few moments she spoke. Within three minutes she had asked the following questions: What is this a picture of? Why did you draw a picture that is so violent? Why are these people fighting each other? Who is going to win? Do you want them to win? Why do you want them to win? Do you think war is good? Do you like to draw?

When she left, the child sat silently for a few moments and then stacked his pencils and crayons neatly and waited. After she finished her rounds she returned to the front of the room. From there she passed out sheets of lined paper to each student. She then gave the assignment, "I want you to write something about your drawing on the paper I just passed out."

My artist friend was devastated. He spent the next five minutes doing everything he could to avoid the paper that lay before him. Finally he started to write but by then the lesson was over. He had hardly gotten a title on the paper. What he had written was,

the wers of Zagod.

A week later I returned to the class and the teacher was continuing with what had now become a daily ritual: draw a picture-write a story; draw a picture-write a story. Almost without being asked the children were woodenly scooping up the pencils, crayons and paper and carrying them to the desk. Again I sat next to my former artist-partner. He drew a simple flower with cottonball clouds in the sky. Even before the teacher had asked, he had begun to write a paragraph about the picture. I said to him that this picture was not as exciting as the first one had been. He looked at me and said "I'm not gonna draw nuthin' I can't spell."

Reflections:
The incredible number of questions the teacher asked the student about his art work was the most sure-fire way ever invented to create a defensiveness about the effort. But even more significant was how the teacher's questions forced the child to fit into her value postures. These are the kinds of questions parents ask of children at the dinner table. I have come to call these thinly-disguised interrogations, "Dinner Table Intero-doctrinations."

The declarative could have been used here with great effectiveness. Examples of statements that might have elicited disclosure instead of defensiveness might have been as follows: I don't know if this is a picture of Earth or of another planet. I think the "bad guys" are in trouble. I always wanted to live in a dome. When I was little my brother used to draw war pictures. I have wondered what it would be like in a war, etc.

This "draw a picture-write a story" lesson is one of the most popular in the elementary schools of this country. It follows the tradition of publishing large numbers of illustrations in children's books. Authors, publishers and teachers know how effectively images communicate ideas. Yet the visual is a fundamental way of knowing. It is an intelligence unto itself. Continuous use of the forms of visual thinking and expression to feed into Symbolic-Abstract codes dilutes both efforts. Teachers and parents are too willing to judge children's worth on their skills with symbols and codes. The result is, as has been said earlier, a diminution of the apparent worth and integrity of visual thought and expression.

The best advice is to provide children with autonomy at least half the time they are involved with visual expression and thought. This means that you ask no questions regarding the work and solicit no justification, explanation or defense of their images. Another tacit honoring of visual expression is to create gallery space for the exhibition of the work. At school, hallways and spaces above chalkboards and bulletin boards have been used quite effectively. (Sorry, parents, the refrigerator door isn't enough.)

Explorations:

Paint a picture that words can't describe.

How does the room look from the inside of a light bulb?

Draw what a kitten sees in the kitchen.

Draw the way people would look if you were underneath the sidewalk and could see through it.

Use five colors of paint and paint forms that say *angry* or *happy* or *shy*.

Choose a word that you don't think you can draw a picture of and then draw one.

Draw what the toast sees inside the toaster.

Episode 2 Music Painting

The children's eyes were closed and whether they were in their seats or lying on the floor, they were all relaxed. The teacher started the music on the tape player. Since the students had done this before, they made no comments or giggles. Often they smiled but it was the private kind of smile that would remain secret.

When the piece had played through, the teacher rewound it for the second playing. Since she had set the tape counter, the rewind went without incident or interruption. The students remained settled and silent. Before the second playing the teacher said quietly, "Watch for images or forms this time. Try to hold onto the most interesting images and we will paint them later." The tape was then played again.

When the tape finished she asked the students again to fix the images in their minds before they opened their eyes. She then said they could go to the art area whenever they felt ready. Some rose at once, others sat or lay still for what seemed an eternity. Finally all were at work. They knew they were not to talk and they painted to the sounds of their own quiet movements, shuffling papers and occasionally running water in the sinks. The paints were liquid—tempera, poster-paint and acrylics. Some used watercolors in cake or patty form. Newspapers protected the tables and the art paper was thick but absorbent.

The images flowed from the brushes, chosen to create big bold strokes. The teacher had set a time limit on the activity so those who had started early had more painting time. The more reflective students who started late had to paint faster. At the end, however, the paintings did not differ in quality. The teacher played the music as the students taped up their artwork in the gallery area of the classroom and again as they cleaned up the materials and prepared for the next lesson. There was no discussion other than the students chatting quietly to each other about their work.

Reflections:
This activity has been used successfully with children as young as three and as mature as eighty. Parents often have to paint with their preschool children just to familiarize them with the media. Once they are accustomed to the media, it is well for the parent and child to paint "back to back" so they don't see each other's work until they are finished.

Many visual artists often hear mental music as they paint. Others have music playing continuously in their studios. Composers like Grofe and Copeland often saw sweeping visual landscapes as they created their symphonic pieces. These two arenas of human wisdom are often inextricably intertwined, with the mind providing the one when the other is absent. To learn to close your eyes and see images and hear music, or to hear music and see images, is a lifelong gift.

The teacher's technique of leaving the experience autonomous is an antidote to the questioning technique used by the teacher in *"The Lost Galactic War."* Strike a happy medium by allowing the students to share their feelings and experiences during the episode. Take care to preserve the autonomy and have the students respond in the first person declarative. That is, have them say, "I feel . . . I sensed . . . I saw," etc. This removes the judgement factor which inhibits further painting or discussion.

Again, display is worthwhile. The gallery can become a place for celebrating images rather than making competitive judgements.

Explorations:

Listen to John Denver's song *"Music Makes Pictures"* and paint the pictures the music makes.

Play different sounds on the piano that represent different colors.

Play music that is just right for a comic book story, a picture in a book, a photograph of grandmother, a car advertisement, etc.

Using the colors to match different sounds, write a song in color.

Play music you think a goldfish would write.

Episode 3 I Didn't Know I Knew That! Words and Images

The mother and father had been scanning the television guide for future shows and had made a list of upcoming specials and documentaries. The ones with the most promise for their plans were on travel and natural history. On the night of one of the special shows, they hung a large piece of paper in the family room to record comments on. After dinner, the family gathered around the paper. One person, usually mom or dad, acted as recorder. The recorder told everyone that the show's topic was "deserts." The family brainstormed about deserts while the recorder wrote all that was said. The list was long and more paper was sought as needed. (Newsprint, the backside of gift wrapping paper and shelf paper can be enlisted.) They took care to record each and every offering without editing. Each family member contributed without question or editorial comment.

After making the list, the family viewed the program, calling out enthusiastically when any "brainstormed" images appeared. Each "score" was loudly cheered and the viewing took on the air of an athletic event.

At show's end, the list was amended to include things that appeared that no one had guessed. This was done in a different colored marker to highlight the things they "learned." Parents helped the younger children re-read their offerings and helped them realize that they knew many things about deserts. Both accurate and misconceived views were noted. They corrected the misconceptions with an attitude of discovery rather than competition.

Reflections:
In classrooms, where the same activity is used with films, the children record their preliminary lists on chalkboards and amend them with different colored chalk. Teachers discourage discussion during the list making, using instead a stream-of-consciousness approach to gain the children's tacit knowings. Later, during the post-viewing time, discussion can make a real contribution.

Avoid "right and wrong" designations; no film or television production is totally comprehensive. For example, a show about deserts may not even mention camels but some child is likely to mention them. This cannot be considered "wrong" but rather right in a different context.

In both classrooms and homes, it helps to have children go to the paper or chalkboard and circle the images they actually saw in the presentation. This helps improve reading skills, memory and spelling and adds a dimension that is missing from Sesame Street. Sometimes it is useful to ask the children to make up a special list of "surprises," things about the desert they never would have guessed.

The purpose of this activity is not to specifically improve reading and writing, but rather to provide children with excursions into their preconscious processes (page 50). Creative people are those who have the greatest access to their preconscious processes.

Explorations:

Make up TV scavenger hunts and see who can fill their list first.

Pick an advertisement from a magazine and find ways to make it contain things you are interested in.

Make up a television show that dolphins would show their young to teach them about us.

Read program descriptions from the TV Guide or your newspaper ahead of time and make a list of ten things you think the show will have in it. As you watch the show, check off the images as they occur.

Episode 4 Concept Portraits
Visual Expression

The room was full of art supplies. There were paints, brushes, pastels, crayons, paper of all sorts, liquid markers, modeling clay, glue, fibers and cloth, woodscraps and even Polaroid cameras. The teacher settled the students into their places and began with the assignment.

He said, "All the materials in this room are for you to use. In a moment I will give you your assignment. But first there are some ground rules. After I give the assignment you will have half an hour to finish. You can talk to anyone here about the assignment except me. Once I give the assignment, I will not explain it further. I will write it on the board so you can be sure what I said *but I will not explain it.*"

By now the room was quiet. The instructor went to the chalkboard and wrote, *"Create an art form that expresses the concept LOVE."* The room buzzed and there were puzzled looks everywhere. Requests for clarification came from every quarter. The instructor merely smiled and pointed to the chalkboard. The frustration level soared.

Finally a few of the class members left their seats and began to gather materials that appealed to them. Armed with various media, they returned to their places and began to paint, draw and sculpt. Almost without exception the first efforts were graphically literal and approached the realm of clichés. Some of these are shown below:

Usually the "cliche'd" art forms were done quickly and the half hour dragged on for those artists who created them. Others, who became engrossed with their materials and the way they chose to express the concept, were seldom finished when the time was up. Occasionally some of the early finishers returned to their art forms and began to embellish them. They took the cliche' they started with and added design features that made the work far more dramatic and complete.

At the end of the lesson the instructor asked the class to display their results in a relatively small area so as to crowd them together and insure that they could easily be seen at once. There was no discussion beyond the remark, "There are many ways to express the concept of love."

Reflections:
Since this was a first-level activity the instructor was satisfied to get the class members to simply paint and sculpt in each other's presence. Discussion after such risk-taking often resurrects old defenses and drives back the value of the visual expression into the embayments of rational justifications. The display element is vital, however, as it forces the class to observe the diversity of expression and experience its legitimacy.

The next level of this activity had individual class members choose a new concept to express through an art form. They had to keep the concept secret. At the end of the lesson the art work was again displayed in a close packed gallery space. The instructor said, "I am going to point to each image and I want you to call out the concept you feel is expressed by the artist. The only person *not* allowed to speak is the artist whose work I am pointing toward."

The result was a marvelous enrichment of meanings for each of the images and forms. The individual often was frustrated by the way so many "misinterpreted" his or her work but at the same time was enriched by the variety of meanings.

A variation on this activity has the class divide into groups of at least five and less than eight. Each group forms a circle and each artist passes his or her image around the circle. Again the original concept is secret. As the art work passes, the person holding it writes on it a phrase the image evokes. The work eventually returns to the artist with five to eight verbal offerings on it. These are presented to the artist as, "things you meant that you didn't know you meant." Often the artist writes a statement about the concept using the collective comments of the other group members. This then can be shared in oral readings.

The activities described above have been used with children as young as three and with adults as well. Of course with the children in home settings the game is often played with a single parent at a time. For our own son, we built a small easel by nailing fibrous wallboard to a wooden box. He had a lightweight portable art stand he could go to on a moment's notice. The wallboard was soft enough to push pins into and firm enough to provide a hard painting surface. Throughout the days at home we would often rush to the easel so he could draw or paint an idea. These images became part of an ever-changing gallery in our hallways.

This exercise has been vital in activities as far-ranging as journal keeping and new product planning in corporate settings. It is a fine access to the processes of the preconscious mind.

Explorations:

Have a painting session in which each person takes turns calling out an "idea" the others have to paint. Each person is allowed no more than five minutes on the first painting and no more than one minute on the last. Decrease the time in proportion to the number of people present.

Do a blindfolded painting and after you are finished have each person decide what the idea is.

Paint a picture of _____'s favorite thing (Donald Duck, Big Bird, Indiana Jones etc.).

Do a mural on wrapping paper or butcher paper at a child's next birthday party. Have each child paint what he or she likes about the party.

Episode 5 Soundsearch

The tape recorder was small and any of the young children could carry it. The cassette tape, pre-recorded by the teacher, contained a sequence of sounds, running for about thirty seconds each with ten-second pauses in between. The sounds were in fact an auditory "map" of a route around the school campus. In each of the stops on the route, there were distinctive sounds so unique that there was little possibility of mistaking them. The task was to have the students retrace the pre-recorded journey with no guidance other than the taped sounds.

This was a beginning lesson and the students were sent out in teams of five. Someone recorded on paper the location of each of the stations. At first the students could use verbal descriptions of each location. On later "sound-searches," they had to use map skills and accurately represent the locations spatially.

As the students became more sophisticated, they chose stations with ambiguous sounds or sounds that could occur at several locations on the campus. This provided an element of uncertainty and required complex reasoning skills. The whole enterprise shifted to a new perspective when the teams were timed in terms of how long it took to complete the course. This introduced a sense of competition that was later turned to cooperation when the winning teams were required to take the other students out and recreate their strategies.

Parents have successfully used the same activity with preschool children in the home. Going from dishwasher to sink to refrigerator and then to flushing toilet keeps many two and three-year-olds occupied for hours. In addition, the young children show remarkable skills in learning to work the tape recorders.

Reflections:

As mentioned earlier, sound and vibration probably activated the first sensory experiences in a child's pre-birth world. The near-total immersion in a world of sound and vibration for nine months provides a potential that often disappears within a few short weeks after birth. Gardner points out that the auditory may well be the first realm of intelligence and the first in which many young children show expertise.

The number of child prodigies in the auditory is remarkably high. All one need do is witness the success of the Suzuki techniques for early musical training and it is easy to become convinced. Many researchers, including Gardner, feel that the ability shown by so many young children is lost as the child grows older. I feel that this may not be the case. The auditory wisdom that a child is born with is probably not so much lost as abandoned. Shortly after birth, children are immersed in a world of auditory logic. That is, they are bombarded with speech and spoken language. This biased ecology of sound narrows their focus, transforming natural wisdom into a refined skill—mastering one's native tongue.

It is surprising how many people have given up their ability to fully listen to the world of sound around them in favor of focusing on speech. Parents start the process by building reward systems around the child's expressions of speech rather than equally honoring patterned non-speech sounds and the unpatterned "babble" that lays the foundation for speech. Schools further the focus on speech with their concern for listening skills. In school, listening skills are those that focus one's attention on the codes and structure of speech.

Activities such as this are invitations to restore the more natural relationship with the auditory.

Explorations:

Create a sound-map of your house.

Find the sounds in your house that are most like music.

Find out which sounds in the house can be heard outside the house. Which outside sounds can be heard inside?

Find out which sounds that you can hear in your house repeat themselves.

Find out which sound in your house recurs the most frequently, is the friendliest, the scariest, the loudest, the softest, etc.

What does your cat or dog listen to in the house?

Find out what the "farthest away" sound is that you can hear.

Episode 6 Music Hunt

The students had been working for nearly a week on the assignment. It was simply: "During this week pay attention to sounds you think are unusual or unique. After you find such sounds, check out a tape recorder and record the sound. Each team (of five) should have gathered five sounds by week's end."

The class had carried out the assignment with remarkable success. They were fourth graders and had learned how to operate the recorders with great skill. They had worked out such things as how long the recording should be, how to avoid background sounds, how to identify their own sounds on the tape ("This is Timmy's team's sound, recorded on Tuesday.") and a host of other operational problems. They were buzzing with excitement because they knew that more was to be done with the sounds.

The teacher led a short discussion about how well they had handled the equipment and the problems that arose from its use. He then had each team play its sounds. Although most teams had been attracted by the same sounds, this overlap actually created a bond between the students.

The teacher then told the students that the last phase of the assignment was about to begin. They now had to put the various sounds together so as to create "music." This caused a flurry of confusion until he went on: "Each of the sounds you have are sounds of the world around the school. What I want you to do is to take bits and pieces of the sounds and put them together without spaces or silent places, so that they make a kind of music."

He then showed them how to use two tape recorders to edit the sounds. One would play back the sounds in the patterns the team-members decided on and the other recorder would re-record the sounds onto a master "music" tape. Gradually they caught on, and soon there were remarkable sequences of sound with different tempos, structures and rhythms. Students from one team would "borrow" sounds from another and soon they discovered that they could play two and even three tape machines into the one that was recording to create hybrid sounds undreamed of at the assignment's outset.

Reflections:

The assignment was remarkably successful in re-awakening students to the worlds of sound around them. But perhaps even more significant was their assembling of original sounds into patterns and structured expression. In effect, this process involved the invention of music.

A secondary reward was the mastery of a fairly sophisticated technology in the form of the tape recorders. The children achieved great success with the tools. Much of this was due to peer teaching rather than intervention by the teacher. In fact, throughout the lesson the teacher encouraged the students to use each other as resources. Nearly all the discussions were aimed at getting the students to know what each team had so far accomplished.

Another primary value of the assignment was that it never involved any form of reading or writing. Most schoolwork concludes with reading and writing, sending the unspoken message that learning experiences are not valid unless they involve reading or writing.

Explorations:

Gather zoo sounds, farm sounds, city sounds, hospital sounds, etc.

Follow various school staff members around and collect the sounds they hear throughout the day. (No voices.)

Record the sound of engines starting up. (Use cars in the neighborhood or teachers' cars.)

Record sounds that do not travel in air. (Put the microphone directly on vibrating surfaces such as pipes, windows, sinks, toilet bowls, refrigerator doors, etc.)

Learn how to record radio and TV shows and film soundtracks.

Learn how to copy records and tapes.

Record a new soundtrack for a movie that is shown in class.

Episode 7 Centering

The class began with the instructor telling the students, "Today we will learn how to do something that doesn't make any sense. There are many things you can do with your mind that you probably don't know about." She cupped her hands over a spot on the desk and asked, "How many of you can close your eyes and let your mind 'look' under my hand?" Most of the students raised their hands.

She then asked them to try. Amid a few giggles there was a remarkable focusing of intent on the task. After a few moments the teacher asked them to open their eyes and tell her what happened. In the discussion that followed it became apparent that "looking" under her hands for most students simply meant imagining whether or not something was on the desk. They had visualized the desk and her hands but had not really "sent their minds" under her hands.

The teacher pointed out that just imagining what was under her hands was not enough. She wanted them to try again. This time she said she didn't want them to try to "see" under her hands but rather to "put their minds under her hands and look out and see the rest of the room as though they were looking about from where her hands were." This activity took a little longer. The children, with their eyes closed, were strangely quiet. This was a different experience for them. After a few minutes the teacher quietly asked them to open their eyes. Once they had done so they began to discuss what was different between the two attempts. Almost at once the children differentiated between "seeing under the teacher's hands" and "seeing *from* the teacher's hands."

One child said it was like when she dreamed and saw herself walking from outside herself. Others said it was "weird" and only a few could not do the activity. The teacher explained that when they had just tried to see under her hands, they sent only their "eyes," but when they tried to see everything from her hands, they sent their minds.

She then asked the students to stand in the commons area of the room. When they had assembled she asked them to place their feet about as wide apart as their shoulders and stand straight. She then asked them to close their eyes and try to see the room around them from their closed eyes. After a few seconds she asked them to open their eyes again. She asked how many could "see" the room. Nearly all the children could do it with ease.

Now she asked the children to put their hands across their "tummies" below their beltline. She showed them by doing so herself. She reminded the students of the activity they had performed earlier, when they had sent their minds to her cupped hands. "This time," she said "I want you to send your minds to the place behind your hands, inside your tummy." Smiles flooded the room. "I want you to see the way the room looks from there." Once quieted, the students began the task. Occasional giggles rippled through the group but clearly the children were involved. Once they had experienced the effect for about half a minute the teacher again asked them to open their eyes.

The discussion that followed indicated that the students "felt" a difference between the two conditions. When they "saw" the room from their eyes they weren't as relaxed as when they "saw" the room from their tummy region. There was a good deal more movement when they were focusing on the cortical or head view as compared with the abdominal or pelvic view. The teacher repeated the activity, asking the students to see from which posture they could "stand still" the best.

She then explained that she was going to test how stable they were and how their minds could help them to be more stable. Choosing one of the students as a model, she asked him to close his eyes and "think about seeing the room from his head." Once he had done so she put her hand on his shoulder and pushed him gently but firmly backwards. He tipped easily and stumbled back into balance. He grinned and the other class members giggled.

She then asked the same student to put his mind in his tummy region. This time when the "push" came, he was extremely steady and stable. There was no tipping or stumbling. He opened his eyes in amazement and the other students gasped in disbelief.

During the next ten minutes, the teacher was able to do the same test with all the students in the class. She also had them do the test with each other, showing them how to push firmly, without overaction. Once they were back in their seats, she explained the difference between putting your mind "high" and keeping it at the "center" of your body. She talked about the center of gravity of the body and how astronauts and space shuttle members learned to move from this center to keep their balance.

This teacher used the procedure daily until all the students could "center" with ease. She used the centering to help settle the students when they became overactive and used it to prepare the students for tests and prolonged tasks. She made it common practice to engage in centering "breaks."

Reflections:

Centering has a long history in esoteric traditions in philosophy and psychology. Many of the so-called Eastern practices of meditation, yoga, martial arts and dance base their traditions on centering. In Western terms, the idea of the center of gravity is useful in explanation.

More difficult for Westerners is the explanation of how the shifting of consciousness from a cerebral-cortical posture to a center-pelvic perspective actually enhances stability. Perhaps this is currently beyond explanation. But explained or not, it works. Accompanying this shift are a more complete state of relaxation, more capability to marshal and direct energy and the already-mentioned capacity for higher physical stability in rest or movement.

Explorations:

Try to center while sitting, running, walking, swinging on the swing, etc.

Center in the shower, at the dinner table, while talking, while watching TV.

Watch your cat or dog and see if they are centered.

Watch your sisters and brothers or classmates and see if they are centered.

Try to teach your mother and father to center.

Episode 8 Centering and Relaxing

The students had chosen partners and were standing in areas free of things to bump into. They took turns checking each other's ability to center. (See previous activity on centering.) This was accomplished by one student (the one doing the testing) standing beside the other. The student being tested stood, eyes closed, with feet about as far apart as his or her shoulders. Trying to think "high" or "cortically," he was tested by the standing partner. The test involves the firm but gentle push on the shoulders that indicates full body stability. See figure below.

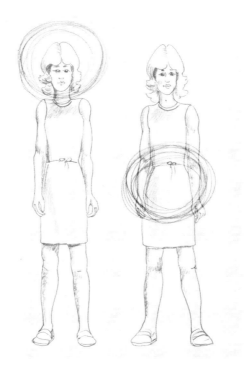

The test was repeated with the students trying to center or think "low" into their abdominal or pelvic region, the locus of the body's "center." Then the students changed places and tried the reverse roles. The next step required that the student being tested choose either the centered or non-centered posture. The partner had to guess which posture was chosen.

In the final series of tests a new element was introduced. The student being tested alternated between being relaxed and being at "attention." (See figure below)

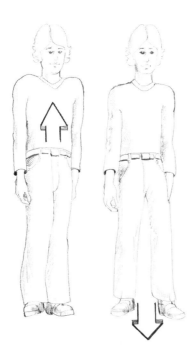

This new element brought the giggles back, along with a sense of exaggerated awareness that the stiffness of "attention" is an extremely unstable posture. The most rigid and most muscle tense postures are also the least stable. The relaxed posture is found to be almost as stable as the centered postures tried earlier. In fact the students discovered quickly that relaxation and centering are probably the same thing.

Reflections:
The teacher helped the students realize that relaxation does not mean "limpness." She showed them that the body has a kind of solidity when centered or relaxed. She also helped them realize that they can't stay centered when being tested if they try to tense up and be "stronger."

Most of us grew up believing that thinking was consciousness, and that to be consciously thinking involved keeping the brain the focus of consciousness. Yet the simple stability check shown through the tests of centering demonstrates that greatest stability comes with relaxation, with consciousness at center. With these experiences, we are ready to explore the use of centering and relaxation as an accompaniment to thinking.

This holistic kind of "preparation" becomes a true expression of kinesthetic wisdom. It is not a skill like writing or jumping. Instead it is a condition which when achieved makes writing and jumping more complete. Some who study these relationships speak of mind-body unity. Mind-body unity is central to the entire concept of kinesthetic wisdom.

Explorations:

Center and relax yourself and write something. Un-center yourself, tense up and write something.

Center and relax yourself and draw or paint.

Center and relax whenever you are given chores to do.

Center and relax when you are hungry.

Center and relax when you hurt yourself.

Center and relax yourself when someone "hurts your feelings."

Episode 9 Centering Everywhere

The students had been given the assignment to keep a record of when they were naturally centered throughout the day and when they weren't. The teacher asked them to pay attention to whether different classes, different subjects and different people were easier or harder to center with. They were also encouraged to see if they could center and relax whenever they caught themselves "off center."

Some of the students wrote their findings on file cards while others just kept them in mind. All were prepared for the discussions when they arose. There was little doubt that centering and relaxation were marvelous criteria by which to judge their daily experiences.

Reflections:
The results were remarkable. The students were amazed at the differences experienced. Some were completely at ease when writing and others were tense and irritable. Some felt tense in art and others cherished the experience. The discussions about whether they were centered or not led to a deep sense of how off-centeredness and physical tension are close partners of feelings of dis-ease.

Even more enlightening were the discussions about whether the students could center in previously non-centered situations. They were quick to cite the role of emotions and beliefs in whether or not they could achieve centeredness. Some students saw the real use of centering as a means for calming down after emotional outbursts.

Teachers and parents who use the methods of centering with children are often impatient and rush the process. In effect they administer centering from a non-centered posture, bringing us to an important premise in regard to this form of kinesthetic wisdom. *It is as important for the person doing the testing to be centered as it is for the person being tested.* The teacher and parent cannot hope to consistently honor centering from a non-centered posture.

Explorations:

Try to stay centered when you have to eat food you do not like.

Maintain center when you are visiting a place you do not want to go.

Remind your parents or teachers when they are off center (*if they give you permission to do so*).

If they do not give you permission, then make sure that you center whenever you are around a non-centered person.

As I learn to center, I learn to better honor my fit in the universe.

Episode 10 Rocking Centered

The child was sitting on the thick carpet of the living room. His father helped him cross his legs and sit with his back straight as shown in the drawing below. Once the child grasped his crossed ankles, the father had him rock backwards until his back was flat on the floor. At that point the father asked the child to try to sit back up again. The boy struggled and tried without success. With a lift from dad the child was brought up to a sitting posture.

The father then asked the child to rock back five or six times until he was comfortable with the motion. Each time the father gently lifted the child again to the sitting position.

Then the father asked the child to try to rock back and then lift himself back to an upright position. The first few attempts were unsuccessful. Sometimes he rolled to the side and other times he would simply struggle and let go of his ankles. On two occasions he lifted himself by pulling on his legs and lunging forward.

After these awkward efforts the father asked the child to think about a large ball resting inside his pelvis. The father said the ball would make the rocking easier if the boy could visualize it being there. He was told to close his eyes and imagine his hips and tummy were inside this "rocking" ball. The father then told the boy to wait until he really felt and saw the ball. When he was ready the father told him he should roll back and up again.

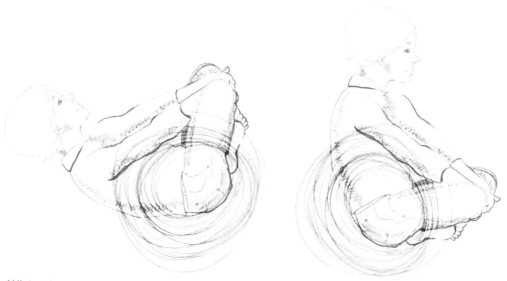

With his eyes closed the child sat motionless for a moment. Then he tipped backward and rolled his back down onto the floor. In a single motion he rolled back up to the sitting position. His eyes popped open in disbelief. But his wide grin made it clear that he knew something had worked. His father smiled too and asked him to try it a half dozen more times.

Now the father asked the child to try it but this time imagine the "rocking" ball was in his head. With eyes closed the child imagined the rocking ball was surrounding his head. When he tipped back he hit the carpet with a thud and there was absolutely no movement upward. Again his eyes opened in disbelief. His father helped him up and asked him to put the "rocking" ball back into his pelvis and try it again. Again the movement was smooth and he easily regained the upright position after rocking back.

Reflections:

This is another approach to centering but, unlike the earlier ones, this activity involves motion. When people are first exposed to the idea that they can focus their consciousness in different places, they believe that they must be still to do so. Yet the ultimate goal of learning to center and place consciousness at our "center" is to have it there at all times. For this reason it is important to learn to center while moving as well.

Recall that the purpose of centering is to establish a mind-body unity and to allow life's activities to take place within the domain of that unity. Thus the child who experiences these concepts early will be less likely to spend non-centered time at home or in school.

A variation of this activity is found in the popular child's game of thinking "heavy" and thinking "light." In this game, one player will "think" about one of these conditions while another tries to pick him or her up. If it "works," the lifting person will sense a remarkable difference between the two conditions: Thinking heavy makes it difficult to pick up the other player and thinking light makes it easy.

Often children will find themselves drawn off center and this activity helps explore the tendency. When children are in the rocking mode and it is successful, the asking of a question can draw them back into cortical consciousness and they will thump to the floor heavily on the next back-rock.

This activity works as well with adults as it does with children. Sometimes when schedules and responsibilities draw me off center, I will find a convenient carpet, beach or lawn and perform the activity for five minutes or so. Occasionally, I will practice difficult parts of a speech while rocking and centering.

Explorations:

Rock while centered and tape record the things that come to your mind while you are doing it.

Learn to rock and turn so you can face new directions at the end of each rock.

Once you have learned to rock and turn, write a poem or song to all the directions.

Episode 11 Earth Bonding

As the teacher watched the children, she noticed remarkable differences among them. Some who were sitting seemed to be floating up out of their chairs. Others seemed to be made of mercury and looked for all the world as though they were sliding in several directions at once. Others were cemented in their chairs as though they were rocks.

The teacher read this scene as ripe for some class activities in centering. Experience had prepared her to sense that the flighty or "light" children were not centered. They were "rising" because they were directing energy upward and seemed to be fighting the earth's natural pull on their bodies.

Children in the "slippery" group were submitting too fully to the earth's pull and weren't maintaining their own strengths. They seemed to be giving their energy and centeredness to all directions at once.

The "rocks" were the only centered ones in the group. They were relaxed, at ease and attentive to everything that was going on. They were far from motionless and their involvement and calming influence seemed to draw others to them. In a way, they were so much what the others wanted to be that they drew the others' centering capabilities away from them. The teacher recognized this and asked all the children to stand.

When they settled down, she asked them to stand as still as they could with their arms at their sides. She invited them to begin a slow rotating motion that let their arms swing in sweeping arcs. At first they tried to hold their arms out like the stiff branches of a tree. She commented that she wanted them to let their arms "flop" and slap against their bodies at the end of the turns in each direction. The figure below shows the movement.

Soon the class had the movement in control and its smoothness became clear to all. The repetition resulted in a dynamic kind of relaxation evidenced by the heaviness with which the children's arms flopped against their bodies. After several minutes the teacher asked the children to stop. She then told them to close their eyes and let their arms rest against their sides. A murmur of responses swept the room, caused by the unusual sensation that arises after doing this activity. The suddenness of the rest after the movement causes the limbs to tingle and evokes a deep sense of the downward pressure of the body's mass.

This is the reaction the teacher wanted. She asked the students to open their eyes and pay careful attention to how the earth was tugging their weight downward. There was no ghost of movement. The entire class was still. She asked them to get a clear feeling of how they felt. She then asked them to sit down. In the discussion that followed, the students spoke of relaxation, peacefulness and feelings of security. Only a few spoke of strange or "weird" feelings and discomfort. These were invariably the ones who showed the greatest degree of non-centeredness.

The teacher then asked them to close their eyes again and to try to experience that downward "pull" while they were seated. With eyes closed, the class, in silence, began forming the same expressions and having the same reactions they had earlier. This time nearly all the students felt the sensation of their own gravitational bonding with the earth.

The teacher used this activity on dozens of occasions throughout the year. This combination of action and stillness was used to precede classroom tests, drill sessions in math, spelling lessons and the standardized tests offered by the school district. The process provided an opportunity for the students to relax and it increased success in test situations.

Reflections:
"Earth bonding" represents one of the most natural ways to center and achieve mind-body unity. Anyone who has driven a car remembers those times when your whole body is raised and seems to be leaving the seat. At the same time, you find your hands gripping the steering wheel and tension rampant in your arms, neck and shoulders. This is an everyday occurrence for commuters, and is also a perfect example of non-centeredness. The driver's consciousness is usually displaced to either the destination or back to the point of origin of the trip. This condition leads to the prime cause of accidents—non-attentiveness.

In classrooms, children are also non-attentive when off-center. However, the non-attentiveness we are talking about here has little to do with "paying attention" only to the teacher. Rather, centeredness provides a greater opportunity to fully experience attentiveness.

Centeredness, then, can be achieved in the three ways so far discussed:

1) by intentionally placing consciousness at our body's center of gravity
2) by relaxing and allowing the body to invite the consciousness to center
3) by honoring the bond uniting our bodies with the downward pull of gravity.

Explorations:

Watch clouds and see if they show centeredness and earth-bonding in different ways.

Watch a stream and determine how it shows earth-bonding and centeredness.

Watch a snake move and see what you learn about centeredness from it.

Determine how centeredness and earth-bonding take place in various hobbies and sports, such as aviation, auto racing, sailing and surfing.

Episode 12 Synergic Math

The teacher was about to introduce multiplication. He told the class that they would be responsible for showing how multiplication worked with art, movement, sounds and numbers. He said that they were to work in teams of three and they could take three periods to plan how they would present the concept of multiplication in a multimedia way four class days hence. Children must use all four modalities in their presentations.

The students had had experience in exploring each modality in different assignments. This was their first attempt toward synthesis. Since they knew about various classmates' special "talents," they formed teams made up of students with differing kinds of expertise. They sought students with different modality skills and differing learning style preferences; students with skills in art, music and dance; those experienced in using different kinds of equipment; and students especially competent in math skills. The teacher became a roving consultant.

As the days passed, activity became intense. The groups focused on their vision of multiplication and attempted to produce skits or minidramas that would accurately portray math concepts. Some adapted lyrics to known popular songs. Others wrote original lyrics to classical pieces (with Beethoven's Fifth Symphony high on the list of favorites). Some designed costumes that had math symbols such as equals (=), times (x), and plus (+). A few groups created posters to decorate sets where the skits were being presented. The whole atmosphere was one of carnival.

As each group presented its conception of multiplication, it became clear that the teams had explored extremely varied facets of the mathematical processes. They treated the "times tables" in auditory cadence while dancing in time. Musically and rhythmically, they explored subtle nuances of number codes. Laughter and participation were high. Each group quickly identified with others and saw at once the logic behind their "art."

Reflections:

After the teams had completed their presentations, it became apparent that far greater sophistication had resulted than anyone could have predicted. Mathematical metaphors of movement, sound and image filled each child's preconscious. They had gained the ability to remember math skills by calling forth the memory of their teams' and classmates' expressions.

The Synergic modality requires cooperation and thus draws people closer together. Each person can draw on his or her strengths in visual, auditory, kinesthetic or symbolic abstract expression. Simultaneously, each child is exposed to competence in other modalities. Peer teaching is rampant.

The Synergic modality is training for life. It transcends the traditionally narrow limits of schoolwork and introduces the skills of lifework.

Explorations:

Create and videotape a multimodal summary of the past year as a holiday gift to each family member.

Create multimodal explorations of how spelling, art, P.E. and history all teach similar things.

Create multimodal expressions of the major problems of the community in which you live.

Episode 13 Scribble Pictures

The teacher was working with Navajo children in their third year of school at Crownpoint, New Mexico. He was seeking an ice-breaking activity that would invite them into playfulness with images and words. After introducing the concept of a "scribble," the teacher drew several on the chalkboard:

The teacher told them that they were going to make pictures out of each scribble. He turned to the board and added lines to transform the scribbles into cartoon-like pictures:

A ripple of laughter greeted the transformation. The teacher then asked two children to come to the board and make a *challenge* scribble for the teacher to work with. The first student made a very conservative scribble:

FIRST STUDENT   SECOND STUDENT

The second would have likely done the same but the teacher encouraged him to make a really "hard" one. The second child added the image to the right. The teacher responded as shown on p. 208.

The students were delighted. The rest of the time was spent with the teacher moving from desk to desk offering *challenge* scribbles and occasionally responding to ones created by the students.

Gradually, color and different media were introduced—chalk, pastel, poster paint, etc. Odd-shaped snips of colored paper were glued down to provide a scribble in a new medium.

Reflections:
The primary lesson in all this is that our brain-mind can make sense out of anything. *Making sense* is what it is designed to do. The use of images and art media in this activity lessened the threat in the cross-cultural setting, yet the same activity has been used with very young children as well as adults past retirement in many different socioeconomic and cultural settings. There is a true sense of play to the activity. It creates a favorable mindset for the *Hidden Meanings* activity which follows and which uses words.

Explorations:

Conduct this activity on long car or airline trips.

Put three ingredients on the kitchen counter and ask your child to cook something using all three.

Have ten or more children create a scribble mural. Each child creates a scribble about three to four inches across, and each scribble must touch another one. Once ten or more scribbles are in place on the mural then the children begin in small groups to choose one and turn it into a picture that makes sense.

Trace shadow patterns on paper and make pictures out of the forms that result.

Episode 14 Hidden Meanings

The teacher asked the students to write a sentence about friendship. The class had been discussing the concept for several days and many of the students had come to a fairly fixed notion of what friendship meant to them. Because of this they found the task simple. The only stipulation was that the sentence have twelve or more words. The teacher wrote one too.

Once they had finished, the teacher asked the students to watch what she was going to do with the sentence. She first wrote it on the chalkboard as follows:

A friend is someone who helps make life more interesting and filled with happiness.

Then she adopted a different format to display the words in the sentence as shown below:

A friend	helps	interesting	happiness
is	make	and	
someone	life	filled	
who	more	with	

The teacher then asked the students to do the same with their sentences. She reminded them to leave open space between the columns. When they finished, she returned to her example on the board. She said that this was a way to say more about an idea than you first intended. She turned to her sentence in its new format and added words in horizontal strands. The words she added plus the words that were already there combined to make *new* complete sentences. It worked as follows:

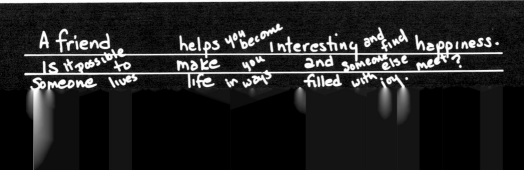

She asked the students to try the same thing with their sentence—adding words they liked which seemed to fit. When the children had finished, they were all buzzing about their new hidden meanings. The teacher pointed out how they could sometimes think that they completely understood something but it might be full of *Hidden Meanings* which were there to invite them to know much more than they knew they knew!

Reflections:
Nearly everyone comes to closure about ideas. Sometimes children who have difficulty writing will effectively imbed an idea in concrete, just to be rid of it. This activity helps develop writing skills at the same time it enhances capacities for understanding and communicating ideas.

Hidden Meanings can be remarkably effective with personal observations and commentary as well. Many adults with whom I have worked have found this activity to be extremely useful in their own journal keeping. The element of randomization helps invite people into new ways of seeing familiar circumstances. It helps people get out of perceptual ruts. It can be used as a way to get an insight and make a breakthrough to solve a stubborn problem.

Explorations:

Use *Hidden Meanings* as a technique to create a class, family or personal project.

Scramble definitions in the dictionary in the same way the sentences were rearranged and make new sentences from the definitions.

Write a single statement or paragraph combining all the headlines on the first sheet of a newspaper.

Episode 15 Honoring Humor

The teacher turned to the class and said, "Benjamin Franklin found that kite flying was an *electrifying* experience." The class groaned. The mother tossed an orange to the waiting boy who said, "Orange you glad I am a good catcher?" Teachers, parents and children are often adept at turning the commonplace of instruction and parenting into a circumstance of humor. In one school I visited, I noted that the children showed a high degree of excitement as the Friday Afternoon Knock-Knock, Giggle and Pun Club reached the appointed hour for their meeting. Their purpose was to share jokes, create puns and write three brand new knock-knock jokes.

Reflections:
The humor that characterized the meeting was a common part of these students' normal experience in the classroom. The teacher had a fine sense of humor and recognized that humor is the commonplace expression of creativity. Just as creativity transforms everyday events into innovative newness, humor disrupts obvious logic into an explosively unexpected turn of events.

Consider the following:

Outside a dog, a book is a man's best friend.

Seems safe enough so far. A seemingly simple literary connection to a mildly chauvinistic homily. The logic is clean and simple. Yet the whole circumstance is tipped into a totally unexpected vein when the punch line is offered:

Outside a dog, a book is a man's best friend. Inside a dog, it's too dark to read anyway.

And so logic is perturbed.

The sudden turn of events that characterizes both creativity and humor is part of an open mind. Closed-minded people are notoriously un-funny. In classrooms and homes where healthy open-system humor is used, children are blessed with an environment that encourages options, flex-

ibility and newness. Closed-system humor (if it can be called that) is notoriously insulting, sexist, racist and ageist. It is in fact negative social or personal comment packaged in a put-down. All one need do is compare Bill Cosby with Don Rickles or Lily Tomlin with Joan Rivers.

Open-system humor is a manifestation of creativity and leads to creativity.

Explorations:

Keep a list of put-down jokes and see how they could be made into non-derogatory humor.

Write humorous captions to put on each of the plants in the home or schoolroom.

Find out how humor is used on television commercials.

Are cats and dogs funny?

Episode 16 Moving To Know

The children were excited and sat with one hand cupped over the top of a fist they had made with the other hand. Their eyes were closed as they listened to the teacher describe the activity they were exploring. The fist was the inside of a seed and the covering hand was the outer skin of the seed. The children were instructed to allow their *seeds* to begin to sprout. They were told to let their seeds grow up into the sunlight.

Their hands squirmed and probed upward into the sunlight of their mind's eye and eventually fingers flared into a depiction of leaves and flowers. When this had happened, the teacher asked them all to stay just as they were and look around the room to see how all the other *seeds* had sprouted.

She then asked the students to show each other what they had done to let their arms and hands represent a seed growing from within the earth up into the sunlight. As they watched each other it became clear that many variations existed. However, each element of each variation had a basis in plant growth. For some the covering hand became the leaves, for others it became the roots. Some argued that the cover was pushed up into the air as the seed grew. Soon it became clear that any single child couldn't, with only two hands, represent what they all knew about plant growth. They formed pairs so one child could represent the "roots" with one hand, the stem with an arm and the other could depict leaves, blossoms and fruit.

Reflections:
The debates and discussions nurtured both cooperation and an accurate depiction of plant growth. But even more importantly, this activity demonstrated the power of the kinesthetic. Once called upon, body wisdom is an important and viable way of coalescing knowledge. I repeated this activity on one occasion with first year graduate students in plant growth and physiology. Their kinesthetic actions and portrayals of sprouting seeds were identical to those of the younger children even though their vocabulary differed markedly.

Explorations:

Move in a way that portrays seven different emotions.

Move in ways that things in the natural world move.

Create a movement zoo, showing how different animals move.

Move in a way that expresses photosynthesis.

Move in ways that show variations in gravity.

Episode 17 Nature Close-Up

The child was invited by her parents to explore the edges of the pond they had taken her to. It was a simple pond, rich in pond life and a temporary haven for migrating waterfowl. Cattails commanded several patches on the shore. Aquatic plants wove a mat on the surface near where a small creek entered the scene.

The adults took all kinds of objects along to the site. They had magnifiers; containers that once held 35 mm film; small, medium and large jars; a net fashioned from cheesecloth, a coat hanger and a broom handle; and several flat, white, styrofoam food trays that provided excellent containers for creatures dredged from the pond bottom.

They began the exploration using the mud at pond's edge. As they searched for tracks and markings left by various animals, the parents showed their approval of the child's natural curiosity and encouraged her to touch, smell and play in each medium they encountered.

They spent a great deal of time in miniature fantasy. They pretended the cattail leaves caught up in the mud were the freeways of a tiny city. They watched the aquatic insects move in and out of the water and envisioned them as residents of the city. Invariably their fantasies were interrupted by a burst of fascination with a diving beetle, a water strider or larval forms clinging to detritus in the pond. Although the parents didn't know what all the life forms were, they showed grace in having the child invent descriptive names like *buzzfly* (dragonfly), *up and down bug* (diving beetle), *water dancer* (water strider), and *dragon in the pipe* (caddis fly larvae).

Birds were noted as they appeared. Creatures caught temporarily for viewing were displayed in the plastic trays. The large jars held tadpoles and frogs for a few moments viewing. Smaller jars allowed them to watch larvae and nymphs which hid around rocks in the pond.

Care was taken to honor the integrity of the life forms. All were treated with "courtesy and compassion." The child was frequently told that, "Today we are learning from the creatures, and treating them as friends—even the strange and scary-looking ones."

Eventually the standard picnic took over, but it was clear—as the child made many trips from the food area back and forth to the pond—that she had made a friend with nature on this day.

Reflections:
Parents as well as teachers are often drawn into recreational use of the outdoors in a fashion that treats the natural offerings of a site merely as a setting. Parks become a place to use playground equipment, have social gatherings and play team sports like softball, volleyball or badminton. Yet there are priceless opportunities for studying nature's riches in nearly all these settings.

Sometimes the obvious attributes such as birds, trees, rocks, lakes and streams are pointed out to the children. Warnings are also frequent, running the range from cautions about drowning to alerting the children to bugs and spiders. The result is a muskox-like retreat to the safety of the lawn around the picnic table. Many parents and teachers like nature if it is fairly large and distant—like Niagara Falls and the Grand Canyon. But tiny, crawly things are systematically avoided.

Plants, animals and humans must now be thought of as. . .a web of related, interacting, dynamic energy systems.
Edith Cobb

Both parents and teachers sometimes share the prejudice that they are solely responsible for knowing all things. They live in mortal fear of having an object thrust upon them that they cannot identify. A parent's ignorance can never justify monitoring a child's experience. The parents described above were not naturalists but they somehow knew that nature held gifts that would benefit their child's life.

Our brain-mind-body system is an offspring of natural systems. All of our senses and sensing abilities grew out of the sweep of natural processes acting over eons. Any visit to nature restores our abilities to be wholly human again.

216

Explorations:

Look at nature "close up" through a microscope.

Make friends with one spot in nature for a whole year. See how it changes each month.

Name the different kinds of clouds you see and find out how many days they appear each month.

Find a spider web that is in a safe place and will not get broken—watch it for fifteen minutes when you have time. Visit it once a week for a month.

Grow five different kinds of plants from seeds.

Moisten some bread and put it in a sandwich bag and let it sit in the dark until some mold grows on it. Make some mold gardens.

Episode 18 Cooperation

The classroom seemed normal in every aspect except one. Everyone was cooperating. There were several gatherings in different parts of the room. One group of students was dampening autumn-dried leaves with a spray bottle. Another group assisted by making a newspaper press to flatten and dry the leaves to remove curliness. Flat leaves were easier to use.

Five different groups of students were working on projects with the flattened leaves. Each group had specific tasks. There were leaf print makers (art), leaf identifiers (science), a shape variation group (math), researchers (language arts), and designers (bulletin board). The teacher had organized a whole lesson around the creation of a bulletin board to display the year's autumn splendor. Each group was working on part of the overall task. The groups were not working in isolation and the teacher encouraged cross-fertilization of ideas.

As each team completed their chosen task, they began to prepare to teach all the other teams the skills they had learned. They knew that the goal of the activity was for everyone to be able to do what everyone else had done.

The teacher moved smoothly from group to group. She was alert to ways to move students with specific skills, abilities and talents into productive contributions. She saw an instance where one girl working on the art phase of leaf printing with brayers, inks and blueprint paper had created mathematically-related ways to position leaves. The teacher asked this student to show what she had done to the variation group. Instantly the math oriented variation group saw a way to display their leaves to maximize the impact of minute differences in shape. With the help delivered, the "consultant" returned to her original group.

The competitive system and premature specialization kill the spirit on which cultural life depends.
Albert Einstein

The activity culminated with a five-faceted bulletin board that included mobiles suspended from the ceiling, a "stained glass" window made of leaves which filtered the autumn light and a host of diverse, tasteful expressions of autumn on the wall itself. Each group had reported what they had done and instructed the other groups in such a way that all could duplicate each other's efforts.

The teacher did not diffuse the joy and excitement that prevailed with attempts to grade the childrens' contributions. Instead she emphasized the excellence that came from cooperation and the students' success in expressing "autumn."

Reflections:
Cooperation is a more effective teaching-parenting practice than competition. In spite of our reflexive tendency to compete, there is a large body of research data that testifies to the limitations of competitive approaches.

In education as well as corporations the role of competition is indefensible. Much of the status of competition is based upon social mythologies created during the dawning and implementation of the industrial revolution. From a mis-reading of Charles Darwin's phrase, "the survival of the fittest," came the idea supported by social Darwinists that competition is "natural." Contemporary biologists and naturalists have all but abandoned that view.

Cooperation is the natural condition. The aberration of competition is a *social* not *natural* contribution. Competition requires score-keeping and thus has been appealing to those whose motives are bonded to quantifiable experience. Schools and industries have demonstrated a history of such ideas but are now beginning to recognize that productivity, quality and mental health are favored by cooperation rather than competition.

Cooperation is the fundamental expression of how the brain-mind system works. Parents and teachers who honor cooperation create experiences compatible with the design of the brain-mind system.

Explorations:

Keep a journal that records situations of competition and situations of cooperation. Determine for yourself how they make you feel.

Find ways that you can cooperate with someone without their knowing it.

Find five "teaching situations" around the home in which cooperation helps. For example: cook a cooperation stew; create a cooperation "beauty" area of plants, figurines or stones, in a place where it can be seen; have all family members design a party that celebrates something ordinarily not celebrated (like next Tuesday) and have them all designate a role for themselves.

Episode 19 Risk

The teacher gave the following instructions:

- On these 3 x 5 cards write down some activity that you are uncertain about or fearful of doing. Pass these in.

- I (the teacher) will read each activity to you and if you are honestly good at doing that activity raise your hand. I will write all the students' names who raise their hands on the back of the card.

- You must look over the list of resource people listed on the backs of your cards and schedule some time to learn how to be comfortable with your resource partner's skills.

Inevitably, several resource experts surfaced for each arena of discomfort. Examples were, "I am afraid of skateboards," "I don't like snakes," "I am uncomfortable with homework," and "I am afraid of junior high school kids." The teacher then had the students choose experts on a "first come/first served" basis and guided them into consultation meetings where the students could gain confidence. The students were told that they had to work together until they gained enough confidence together to *risk* trying the uncomfortable or fearful activity.

Reflections:
Complete resolution of the fear was not the issue, although it most often happened. Rather the issue was to get people to blend confidence with compassion and weave discomfort with courage.

Peer teaching and peer instruction is a powerful way we all learn. Activities such as these bring the words *risk, courage, fear, discomfort, confidence*, and *compassion* into the language of teaching and parenting.

Explorations:

Address three fears that you have, all by yourself.

Make a fear chart with two columns. One column should contain fears you used to have but no longer have and the other column should contain fears that you still have. Keep a record of ones you lose and new ones you gain.

Make a list of ten risks you are willing to take in the next year. Keep track of how many you actually address.

Find out the relationship between fear and understanding.

What we need is a generation of students who are fearless in the face of the tentative.

Episode 20 Peace Close-Up

The teacher sat crosslegged in front of the gathering of fourth grade students and asked them what kinds of things would increase world peace. Immediately they began offering such suggestions as "Get rid of all the bombs," "Fire the armies," "Sign some papers and make war against the law." The teacher rose to note each offering on the board. Once the list was complete, she sat again with the children and asked them if there was anything like war in their lives.

They were puzzled at first but eventually they seemed to begin to realize that the teacher meant *war* as a metaphor. One student said, "My brother declares war on me when I bother his things." "My Dad blows up at bad drivers," offered one girl. Another said she did war with one of her deceitful friends.

Eventually the thought emerged that all violence was in conflict with the idea of peace. Through the discussion the teacher introduced the concept that they could decrease violence and enhance peace in their own lives by giving up the "fighting stance" with brothers, sisters and other people. She asked them to spend the rest of the week keeping track of the times when they chose to implement peace instead of violence.

My moments of greatest happiness were when I lost myself all but completely in some instant of perfect harmony.
Bernard Berenson

By the end of the week the students had experienced dozens of instances where violence and conflict had been avoided in their personal lives. The father who lost his temper at other drivers had felt support from his daughter whenever she rode with him. On one instance she complimented him for how well he avoided another driver and consoled him when he had lost sight of a motorcycle and barely missed forcing the cyclist off the road.

Eventually the class created a peace movement in the school. They helped re-write school rules that nurtured conflict; e.g., you cannot play four-square when people are playing basketball and vice-versa. (The four-square courts were painted inside the basketball courts on the playground.) Loaner bicycles were designated so students without bicycles could learn to ride. Homework became more inventive with drill and rote activities being done in supervised quiet time. Parent-teacher meetings always started with input from students (a dance, a skit or an art or science exhibit). Cooperation became the primary path to see peace "close-up."

Reflections:
Children (and nations) often resort to violence because they do not believe they have options or can make choices. Recognizing options and making choices creates experience compatible with our design. It is all too easy to discuss, analyze and evaluate grand abstractions like, "Who was right in the Civil War?" Yet until the notion of options and choice is woven into the fabric of daily life, little is realized about the intimacies of war and peace.

Peace is too important an idea to remain an abstraction.

Explorations:

Find out the difference between playing *hard* and playing *dirty.*

Watch a few televised football games with a parent and discuss the events in terms of *peaceful* competitiveness and violent *warlike* competitiveness.

Find out where *war* and *peace* are to be found in your communities.

Visit an art gallery and classify the art objects as to whether they are warlike or peaceful.

Find out what peaceful things you *cannot do.*

Make a tape recording of paired examples of violent music and peaceful music.

The open mind does not deny convention
it merely uses convention as a starting
place for original exploration.

THE EDGES OF KNOWING

KNOWING

PART VI

The Edges of Knowing

An open mind can add, subtract and spell with grace. It can express respect, dignity and compassion. It can honor law and order along with perfect attendance at the voting booth. An open mind can find its way to church on each day of worship and serve on jury duty. The dominant way it differs is that—unlike the closed mind—it sees these activities as *chosen and preferred options* rather than absolute criteria of enslavement to cultural expectations.

The closed mind is the mind of bigotry. It has the reflex to imprison itself within the central region of an all-pervasive and unquestioned "truth." There it lies in fearful anxiety about those "evil" tendencies toward change that lie on the other side of a self-inflicted perimeter beyond which it refuses to look. Just as surely as the enslaved mind refuses to see the possibility of change in the structure of accepted order, it refuses to see its own capability to function in ways the external order denies.

George Leonard tells the story of a rural midwestern girl who while washing dishes one stormy summer evening was thrust to the boundaries of her mind. She was standing at the sink watching the flickering roll of lightning over the wheat fields that swept from the horizon to the edge of her yard. As she washed the dishes she felt a strange sensation first chill and then warm her.

As she looked out onto this misty dance of the atmosphere, she became engulfed in knowing that this was all part of her. She knew that all the things she witnessed were her and she was another place in its limitless form. The awareness locked her motionless. Her eyes stared at the horizon without looking at any specific object. She could not remember how long she stood there, but the reverie was broken by her mother who became quite alarmed at her state. Disturbed even more by her daughter's explanation, the woman drew her husband into the growing circle of anxiety.

That night as the daughter slept the parents decided to take the girl to town and visit the family physician. The next day this was done. The parents briefed the doctor and quite appropriately he found the girl's behavior "strange" enough to refer her to a psychiatrist in a neighboring town. After a lengthy examination, the doctor encouraged the family to allow the daughter to voluntarily commit herself to an institution for the mentally disturbed.

After eighteen months the young woman dis-enrolled herself and moved to central California. Bewildered by knowing that she was still deeply convinced of this sense of unity, she remained wracked with guilt and shame about the pain she had caused her parents and childhood friends. Eventually she made a new life for herself and even had the courage to share the story in a public forum.

This woman was lucky. A hundred years ago she would not have had the privilege of "voluntary" commitment. She would have been remanded to the madhouse for life. Two hundred years ago she would have been burned at the stake. All she did was to pay attention to something her brain-mind was doing in its interaction with the world.

Just as Pribram defined consciousness as "what we pay attention to", culture defines the limits of that attention zone. The limits of the mind's propriety are now so externalized as to have become legal rather than medical. The illegality that we call crime is often the behavioral expression of the mind. Consider the act of protestation. If one marches in a rally the act is legal if there is a permit for the rally. It is illegal if there is not. If one burns a person in effigy the act is usually accepted. If one burns a Boy Scout flag there will be little repercussion. However, burning an American flag will send one to jail.

In courts of law the expert testimony of psychiatrists and psychologists is becoming less acceptable as legal evidence. Why? Because there is so little agreement and legal precision in the testimony. The mind changes but the law does not. In a sense contemporary mind function is being entombed in archaic and outdated expressions and institutional meanings. Definitions of mind are not sufficiently established to fit into formal governance procedures. And how thankful we should be that they are not. The ultimate form of totalitarianism would be an agreed upon legal definition of mind.

The mind is simply wider and more comprehensive than any definition of it, legal, psychological or medical. The concept of open-system consciousness is becoming more pervasive than the notion of closed-system definitions. The result is that we are ushering in an era of unprecedented freedom for the mind. There is growing evidence that institutions are beginning to broaden their perspectives. Our minds are being democratized by the information era. Television provides thousands of times more information per month than we received in our entire formal schooling. The difference is that the information is multimodal and thus more holistic. Computers are taking up residence in our homes and as amplifiers of the brain-mind system are giving us the power to access knowledge far beyond educational institutions. A new freedom of mind is being born. This freedom will be expressed by each individual and will extend rapidly beyond the limits imposed by the shackles of antiquated closed-system vision.

The medical establishment is already re-honoring the role of the mind in healing. Holistic medicine is the most rapidly growing application of open system thought in contemporary society. Books, articles, films and video programs about the widening explorations of the brain-mind system are growing in popularity and credibility. Workshops and seminars about research in the neurosciences are attended every month by thousands of people from the non-medical community. Industrial and corporate management are successfully and enthusiastically using new approaches based upon neural research.

The educational community, experiencing a similar renaissance, is deeply immersed in accessing information and approaches spawned from neuroscience. Although some school systems are regressing, many others are evolving in innovative ways. They are systematically applying learning modality and learning style approaches similar to the ones described in these pages. Others are exploring creativity, lateral thinking, problem solving and diverse innovations such as flexible scheduling and community action programs. Overall, I am heartened that so many have shown the courage to honor a broader conception of the brain-mind system. I hope for ourselves and our children that we choose to utilize this knowledge.

Again and again, step by step, intuition opens the doors that lead to man's designing.
R. Buckminster Fuller

In the next pages we will explore some of the more remote modalities of the brain-mind system: sleep dreaming, synchronicity, *deja vu*, precognition and prescience. These are ways of knowing that many dismiss and often ridicule. Yet people we work with report that these "edge" modalities have changed their whole concept of "normal" mindwork.

Night-Dreaming

Recently Nobel Laureate Francis Crick claimed that night dreams are the brain's way of erasing useless information and experience. Crick's area of expertise is the structure of genes, and he co-discoverered the structure of the DNA molecule. His statement could be left to rest if it weren't for his reputation in a field far from the study or even utilization of dreams.

Serious students of dreams are so convinced to the contrary that many would not even be drawn into challenging his claim. Dream researchers and tens of thousands of people who pay attention to their dreams testify to the value of dreams and the dream state. My own interest in dreams came with my work with Richard Jones and Margaret Donaldson, mentioned in the first chapter. I can think of little else that has offered me such consistent enjoyment or has contributed more to my work in writing, film-making and public speaking. Crick's views come clearly from a reductive materialist posture from a person who has disregarded the dream reflection process.

I have dreamed the detail in all the films I have made. The most recent example was the film I made with colleague Robbie Porter for the Southern California County Superintendents of Instruction. The film was titled *To Honor Art*.

During several meetings and phone calls we established the main flow of the film. After all the input and rational discussions, I rented a room at Laguna Beach and began the process of intentional dreaming about the content and form of the film. One afternoon and one early morning session were sufficient. On the second day before breakfast, I took pad and pencil to the beach and by ten o'clock I had the first complete draft of the shooting script. The shooting script is a detailing of all the images, narration and suggestions for the technical fades, cuts and dissolves. In the month that followed, fewer than twenty word changes were made in the production of the script.

The researchers tell us that as much as twenty percent of our lives may be spent in the dream or REM (Rapid Eye Movement) state of sleep. They also tell us that intentional deprivation of the dream state causes psychotic symptoms within seventy-two hours. For a hundred years therapists have used dreams to help clients search out significance in their perceptions. Before that, the shaman and soothsayer joined a priestly crowd that considered dream experience as an even more special condition than reality.

With small children, dream sleep is the world of remarkable adventures. Unborn children dream in utero. Children in the early stages of toilet training often gain from dreams permission to wet the bed. In the dream they find themselves on the toilet or in the shower, tub or swimming pool. One man, near seventy, told me of an elaborate dream he had had as a child. In his dream his parents were always off on an old-fashioned river boat. They inevitably went on board before he did, resulting in his running to the dock and leaping across the space between the dock and the departing boat. He failed each time and when he struck the water he would wet the bed. He stopped wetting the bed when he stopped missing the boat.

Richard Jones taught me to systematically harvest my dreams fifteen years ago at a conference I directed in the Colorado Rockies. The first few of these conferences (the Solstice Seminars, funded then by the federal government) were aimed at developing leadership in broad-based groups of educators. I have continued to utilize Jones' methods in all the years since he first introduced me to them. The seminars are now open-enrollment experiences designed to explore methods to hone open-mindedness. Dream reflection is central to the offerings.

Dream Harvesting

STEP 1: *Place a pad and pen or pencil near your sleeping place.*
Writing the first few dreams down is a must. Beginners are always surprised how easily the content of dreams is lost, even of the vivid ones.

STEP 2: *Before going to sleep, close your eyes and remind yourself that you are going to try to harvest a dream by carrying out the steps that follow.*
Many consider this step a form of self hypnosis or auto-suggestion. All beginning dream harvesters who try it are convinced it is invaluable.

STEP 3: *Go to sleep.*
As simple as this sounds, there is more to it. Many people do not pay attention to falling asleep. For example, few know that there is a quality of sleep called pre-sleep that we go through before entering the deeper forms of sleep. As one becomes more experienced in dream harvesting procedures, the pre-sleep period becomes a useful one for daily problem solution.

STEP 4: *Dream!*
Again, with slight tongue-in-cheek, this seems too simple. However, when you drift into the dream state your brain irrigates itself with so much blood that the body cannot maintain muscle tone. The deepest relaxation that one ordinarily experiences is at this time. Experienced dream harvesters are aware of this shift in body state and use it as a cue that dreaming is beginning.

STEP 5: *Pay careful attention to the dream. Note colors, smells and special experiences such as flying, being chased, fear and humor.*
This may seem impossible to beginning dream harvesters. In fact many will be satisfied if they simply are able to be sure they had a dream. However as they explore the process they will find an amazing leap in their ability to attend to detail.

STEP 6: *At the end of the dream WAKE UP! Once you begin to wake, KEEP YOUR EYES CLOSED.*
This is perhaps the most difficult step in the whole process. The normal tendency is to drift into deep sleep upon completion of a dream, except during early morning or waking dreams when sleep is done for the night. As a result, many new dream harvesters will find it easier to carry this step out with morning or "alarm clock" dreams. Mastering this step is important, though, since rich dreams often occur early in the sleep cycle. Learn to harvest these as well.

STEP 7: *With your eyes closed, review the key elements in the dream. Once these are reviewed, open your eyes and record the few words that capture the essence of the dream.*
The reason one must keep his or her eyes closed is to avoid the visual "erasure" caused by seeing the distracting images in the sleeping place. If the dream images remain, they are easily reviewed and can be written down. These recordings need not be elaborate, just a few words will do.

STEP 8: *Return to sleep. Steps 6 and 7 may be repeated as often as you choose throughout each night.*
For beginning dream harvesters, recording a single dream often is reward enough. Although experienced harvesters may not record every dream, they often wake up, review the dream and "catalogue" it for later examination. *Beginning dream harvesters should not try this "cataloging."* Record only the key words at first. Many dreamers who believe their dream was so vivid they could never forget it wake in the morning with absolutely no recall of the dream.

STEP 9: *In the morning, review the key words and elaborate in writing all that these words mean to you as you describe the dream. Stick with good journalistic descriptions rather than interpretations.*
Here the attempts to capture a dream are fulfilled. At first this is an awkward step. Sometimes a person will not have the slightest idea of the meaning of the many words that were written down. Others will have written them on top of each other as they recorded them and will find it impossible to read them. But for most, if the words were recorded the connections will pop back into consciousness sometime during the day. One should try to complete the process when this happens. The written elaboration may take the form of a few sentences or, as has been true in my case, it may result in a film or an entire article or parts of a book.

These same steps were used by Richard Jones when he served on a multidisciplinary team of faculty members in a "Dreams and Poetry" program at The Evergreen State College in Olympia, Washington. The program attracted first-year students whose eventual writing quality far exceeded expectations. The students became involved in three phases of study.

The first phase was to study writers whose work was thought to have been strongly influenced by dreams. These were Dante, Melville, Shakespeare and Chaucer. The second phase was to learn to harvest dreams and turn them into a variety of written forms. The last was to discuss both their own writing and the literature of these masters.

Although "Dreams and Poetry" was offered to first-year college students, I have used similar approaches with fourth grade students and older. Children as young as three years are extremely adept at recalling and discussing their dreams. I have had young non-writers make a dream sculpture with soft plasticene (oil-based) clay rather than writing things down. Later they bring the sculpture to me, close their eyes, hold the sculpture in their hands and recall what they dreamed.

Instructional Uses of Dreams

Since the topic of dreams can awaken rather remarkable and occasionally negative reactions in some sectors of the community, I recommend the following rules.

1) Explain to your students that a great many of the immortal writers wrote from their dreams. Let them know that many visual artists and film-makers do this as well. Many scientists have credited dreams for providing solutions to complex academic problems.
2) Explain that there are steps one can take to help remember and record dream experience. Share with them the steps listed above.
3) Have the first few assignments be simple and non-threatening such as "See if you can see color in your dreams", "See if you can change what is happening in a dream" "See if dreams are related to what happens during the day" "Find something in a dream that you can paint a picture of."
4) When the children are reporting their attempts at carrying out the assignments, make sure they are never questioned about the dream experience. Protect their privacy. All that should be reported is fact and description. No attempt to engage in "therapy" or to search for meaning should be allowed.

These are rules for the students. I feel it is necessary to inform parents of the value of dream reflection in writing and art. This is a good place to mention Shakespeare, Dante, Melville and Chaucer. Most are comfortable with the use of dreams for such a purpose. In my experience most parents are comfortable with the scientific study of dreams as well. Thus, a great many elements of dream study are perceived of as valuable and valid. Many of the classic research studies, such as dream transmission and the dreaming of a target image, are useful. Nearly all parents are comfortable with the instructional uses of dreams. They are understandably less comfortable using dreams therapeutically or to explore family issues.

Dream Options

As the process of recording and elaborating their dreams becomes easier, students are ready for a class activity with a single dream. When giving an assignment to attempt a harvesting for that night, explain that written elaborations are required because the class will do something different with the dream the following day. Encourage good descriptive narrative with no interpretation.

When the students come back to class the following day, explain the ground rules. One volunteer who has prepared a fairly complete narrative will read it to the class. While the reading is taking place, the other students will sit, relaxed, with their eyes closed, and treat the experience like a guided imagery. They will be responsible for remembering their personal reactions to the reader's descriptions and images. The reader will be cautioned again to avoid any interpretations or explanations.

Once the reading is complete, allow the students about two minutes of silence in which to organize their thoughts. After the preparation time they will begin to offer their reactions to the images provided. Remember to insist that they speak in the first person singular. *They are recounting their images and their interpretations after all; the narrator is to be protected with complete immunity*. This prevents abusive questioning, teasing or ridicule from other classmates. Such actions are rare and if they occur are usually early on in dream study. Students quickly recognize the benefits of dream reflection and treat the experience responsibly.

The teacher should record the students' offerings in short metaphorical summaries on the chalkboard. An example might be as follows:

> Susan, a sixth grade student, read her narrative of a dream from the previous night. Her dream was rich in images about the sea and a coastal village in New England. It involved a search for a missing box that was possibly a jewel case. After a lengthy search in which she received erroneous instructions as well as some that were fairly useful, she recovered the box to find that it contained only dried flowers. She was so surprised that she awoke.

At the end of the reading, the class sat quietly for about two minutes, forming their own images from Susan's input. When the period of reflection was over the teacher spoke. "O.K. class, let's hear from you." She reminded students to speak in the first person and to speak as though it was their dream and not Susan's. The first commentary was as follows:

I was a famous detective working for old Mrs. Gladmoney. She had hired me to find her missing valuables. It took a long time because some creeps in town hoped I wouldn't find the jewels and that would give them a chance after I gave up. Other people who knew Mrs. Gladmoney were honest and tried to help. Finally I went into a dark tenement house by the wharf. Suddenly a man grabbed me from the rear. Quickly I remembered all my karate training and when he stopped rolling he was out cold. I heard a door close down the hall. I ran to the door and opened it to see a figure leap out the window and to the roof below. When he hit the roof he hurt his leg and that made him drop a small package. I followed him out the window and was about to go after him when I noticed that the package was about the size of the jewel box. I opened it and it was the box. I went quickly to Mrs. Gladmoney and she was incredibly relieved. She told me these were the flowers from her wedding bouquet. She had a tear in her eye as she paid me double my usual fee. I felt good as I left.

The teacher thanked the boy and wrote the following on the board:

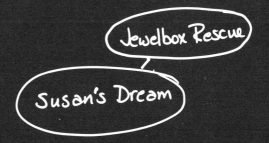

When as many as wanted to had offered their interpretations, the board looked like this:

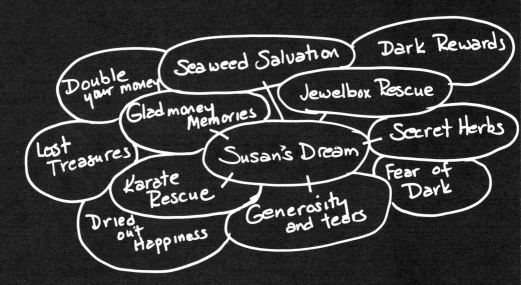

Throughout the process, the teacher tried to capture the essence of each offering. She condensed the narrations into four-and five-word capsules. At the end, with twenty options on the board, she pointed out to the class that dreams mean almost anything you want them to. Dreamers who come to a single conclusion about the meaning of a dream often lose the opportunity to explore a variety of possiblities.

Dream Drama

Drama is an arena that lends itself to excellent dream exploration. The dreamer is the director, playwright and casting manager. Once the cast is assigned, members are allowed artistic license to freely interpret their roles.

The actors can be invited to describe how the character looks and sounds. If a part had no dialogue in the actual dream, it can be added later. Dialogues muttered to one's self enrich a dream play immeasurably. Art work in terms of set design and even a musical score can be proposed for the play.

Dream Gallery

A remarkably dramatic use of dreams is the creation of multimedia expressions of the images, feelings or content of dreams. Often the images are far more mature than those students create in their art classes. If the student becomes adept at dream harvesting, he or she will augment art work with floor plans, architecture, fabric quality, clothing design and sculpture.

Dream Heroics

Once students are skilled at dream harvesting,they may safely attempt the following activity, which involves chronicling fearful dream experiences. When beginning dream harvesting, both adults and children report and seem to have the greatest recollection of fearsome dreams.

The reason is quite simple. Recall the step in the dream harvesting process that requires you to wake up. This is the step that helps anchor the dream in waking consciousness. It is also the step that prevents you from dropping into deeper sleep states which erase the dream content. As hard as it is for beginning dream harvesters to learn, it is a step they already know quite well. *Frightening dreams wake you up whether you want to be woken or not.*

What we want to do with fearful dreams is to have the dream harvesters stay asleep. While in the regular dream harvesting process, the subject learns *intentional waking* to record the dream. With the fearful dream, *we want the subject to fight the "fear" or waking reflex and stay with the frightening dream.*

One of the things we now know about dreams is that *the dream experience is real experience.* The advantage of this reality is that it does not create real injury. By confronting danger, fear, injury and even death in dreams, one can develop a more realistic way of confronting the same circumstances in waking life. Many teachers and parents have noted distinct heightening of self esteem and self image in children following a regimen of confronting dream fears. For children I have worked with, the dream state has become as rich and useful a part of their life as their waking state. They become so tuned in to dream experience that they sometimes question whether they experienced something in a waking or a dream state.

Good Dream Journal

Although we tend to have the best recollection of the frightening dreams or nightmares, most dreams are pleasant or at worst bland. These are definitely dreams that would not wake you on their own. As a result, the dreamer usually drifts into deep sleep and loses the dream. The harvesting process allows the dreamer to explore the gentler dreamscapes as well as the fearful ones. Even the most innocuous dream is rich for the experienced harvester.

A worthwhile assignment for beginning dream harvesters is to record and remember the next few good dreams, ones in which there are pleasant and happy circumstances. As they do this, they often experience an attitudinal shift about dreams and become far less apprehensive about their occurrence.

Summary

Dreams do not represent a separate form of reality. They are part of the same reality that the brain-mind-body has evolved to explore its passage within this world. To ignore these explorations is like denying our senses or the variety of ways we process experience.

Awareness of dreams simply increases our options. By greeting them as allies in the process of honoring our consciousness, we move into a realm of experience central to our design.

Sensing From Mind's Edge

One of the most puzzling, yet common, phenomena of mind is our ability to suddenly and completely sense a pattern of events or conditions without consciously thinking about it. Sometimes the awareness takes the form of what we call coincidence, where an unexpected juxtaposition of objects and events in space and time shocks us into noticing them. This juxtaposition may be as simple as finding a parking place in front of the site of a late appointment, or the sudden location of a set of lost keys. Psychologist Carl Jung called this synchronicity rather than coincidence. He felt that it represented a harmonic resonance rather than accident.

In more complex forms of knowing, you may sense complete familiarity with a setting or circumstance when you know you have never been there before. This is an example of what is called *deja vu*. Another, more holistic, form occurs when you enter a setting and become aware that you know everything that is about to happen. And as surely as if they were scripted, the events unfold on cue. This pattern is called *prescience*. Another more disconcerting form of prior knowing is the gnawing awareness of something that is going to happen in the future. This is called *precognition*.

Each of these forms of knowing is greeted with doubt and skepticism, even in the field of psychology, where such body-mind experiences are classified as *para*psychology. Remember that para means "along side of" or "beyond." Those who experience these forms of knowing with any frequency are labelled psychics, mystics, seers, clairvoyants, readers, fortune tellers, mediums, soothsayers, oracles and charlatans. Seldom are these talents looked upon with favor.

Our culture creates an aura of denigration and ridicule preventing acknowledgement of those forms of knowing without awkwardness or embarrassment. We neither sanction nor provide an adequate vocabulary for such forms of knowing. Without a vocabulary we tacitly begin to deny the experience.

In the past, it was easy to confuse the expression of the experiencing of *synchronicity, deja vu, prescience and precognition* as the lamentations of mental illness. To assign insanity to whatever a culture does not permit as accepted mindwork has been the definitive path of history. The most intimate of repressions have been the repressions of mind.

We now know that there is much validity, although not much socially-honored legitimacy, to the realm that is labelled *parapsychology*. Each of us has experienced things contemporary psychology cannot explain. But the lack of an explanation can never deny the experience. Somehow I feel that this is changing. Some of the models we are exploring to account for the natural workings of the brain-mind system are beginning to justify those knowings once called parapsychology.

Within just a few years our understanding of the mind will soar. Soon we will allow ourselves to slip the bonds of the archaic thought and convention that we cherish. A perfect example comes to us from the realm of physics. For nearly two hundred years our vision was limited by the mechanical laws of Isaac Newton. Once we moved away from the overwhelming presence of Newtonian physics, we were permitted a galaxy of discoveries formerly locked away by our closed methods of thinking. As we removed the barriers to perception, we began to understand the world in a new way.

My intent is not to attack the ways of science and its methodologies, but to support the notion that in our universe closed-minded ideas are doomed. Truth has no dominion in science, in spite of the romanticism of much scientific literature. *Honesty* rules science. Thus we have a built-in, although inefficient, guarantee of the continuous evolution of thought.

One of the ideas challenging the rigidity of scientific closedness is currently championed by British scientist, Rupert Sheldrake. Strangely, if Sheldrake's ideas prove to have merit, we may be the beneficiaries of a physical model that explains *all* the forms of mindwork discussed above. Sheldrake is the most vocal proponent of a family of ideas based on the concept of *morphogenesis*. Morphogenesis literally means the origins of form.

Morphogenesis is concerned with how things arrange themselves in such consistent patterns that quartz crystals found on the moon are exact replicas of ones found on earth. It is related to any number of fields ranging from subatomic structures to the structure of behavior and thought.

Sheldrake holds that whenever structural order is created in a given substance, a resonance pattern is also produced. This resonance pattern then produces conditions that act as a structural template that guides the formation of other similar substances. He calls this pattern-inducing structural template a *morphogenetic field*.

What all this translates to is that when something happens, and happens over and over again, the likelihood of its continuing to happen in that same way is increased. It doesn't seem to matter if the event is the formation of a crystal or the configuration of a thought. Although this concept is being challenged by the scientific community, it has received remarkable support as well.

The holonomic model of the brain-mind system seems to me quite compatible with Sheldrake's ideas. Perhaps thought is mental morphogenesis. It seems likely that the neuro-electrical patterns created by thought would be in some kind of harmony with patterns configured throughout the natural world. Could it be that we have a yet-undisclosed capacity to "tune in" to morphic resonance? Do these rare moments of "tuning in" produce *deja vu*, prescience, precognition and synchronicity? Could our more common experiences of spontaneous insight and intuition rely on an instantaneous harmony between our inner and outer worlds?

An even more intriguing issue relates to whether or not the form we have inherited through the process of evolution represents countless adjustments between inner and outer harmony resulting in the wondrous capabilities of our brain-mind system. Are we on a threshold of discovery similar to the one that years ago was accompanied by a doubling of cortical size? Are we about to discover how to think in resonance with the cosmos?

What these ideas offer us is not *the* answer but rather a set of possibilities. With morphogenesis and holonomy being considered, many more things have the possibility of explanation. Synchronicity might be the intentional or random "tuning-in" of our minds to the morphic resonance of a particular circumstance. *Deja vu* can be also the expression of an intentional or passive patterning of one's mind to a resonance. Prescience and precognition can be the early sensing of forming patterns.

Other explanations have begun to accumulate as well. A number of writers suggest that such insight is based on past life experiences. Some make claims of alien consciousness and involuntary travel to other worlds. Some have suggested that guides lead us from other worlds, through birth, into this life, and into the worlds beyond death.

But again be clear. Whether these or any other explanations are valid, we *do* experience these ways of knowing. We neither have to deny them because society forbids their legitimacy nor because science is still constructing their models. All we need do is permit ourselves to honor the reality of our own mind's work. Here again, children have the advantage over us. Recall our son's knowledge of the location and carpet color of the apartment I lived in before he was born. Recall the times children in your presence have said things with such passion and conviction that you stood bewildered. Remember they have not been exposed as long as we to the pressures to conform.

So "The Edges of Knowing" is an invitation to intentionally honor those excursions into the farther reaches of mind that children regularly seem to make. We honor them most of all by considering them normal and appropriate. The following activities are a few of the ways my colleagues and I have explored in helping children access these regions of their minds.

Aesthetics is the pattern which connects; reason is that which is connected. The whole mind possesses both.

Deja Vu Journal

Children often speak about "it used to be like this" or "this is how it happened a long time ago." Most often such comments are dismissed by adults as play fantasies. Even when the child persists, he or she often is assured that the idea is just part of his or her imagination.

Adults experiencing *deja vu* report an eerie sensation and a feeling of strangeness settling over them. Sometimes these experiences are related to travel, other times to a pattern of events, such as a meeting, a dinner engagement or a theatrical production. Perhaps the most common expression of *deja vu* is the sensation that you already know a person you have just met or seen.

The *deja vu* journal is simply a place where such experiences are recorded and dated. Many are amazed at the frequency with which these events occur. Subsequent occurrences heighten one's sensitivity and sensory acuity. Knowing the experience will be recorded in journal form expands your awareness and stimulates vivid images and feelings.

Parents need to comfort younger children regarding these events and all the activities in this section of the book. Honestly respect your childrens' minds. Children look to parents to determine what is appropriate mindwork and what is not. Parents who value these ways of knowing treat them as normal, which means no phone calls to neighbors to gossip about what the child has done and no later commentaries to friends in front of the child.

Children can be encouraged to share dreams, premonitions and *deja vu* experiences. Adults can record the events, and even remind the child to "tell mommy or dad about the times you know something you didn't know you knew." The payoff for all this is simply extended awareness— awareness that widens our conception of mind.

Prescience and Precognition

The same procedures may be used for prescient and precognitive experiences. The specific definitions of these terms are not important. "Knowing about things in the future" or "knowing things that haven't happened yet" are often used as working definitions.

Events frequently occur in children's lives that embody these two ways of knowing. The most common is figuring out intuitively the ending of a story, film or TV show. Occasionally this intuition extends to the lives of celebrities and other public figures. When it concerns friends and family members, children often express anxiety and discomfort; they fear "knowing" something in this way can actually *cause* the event to occur.

Dreams enhance our awareness and experiences in these realms of thought. When dream harvesting becomes a reality for children and adults alike, *deja vu*, prescience and precognition experiences occur more frequently. Some might suggest that if these ways of knowing cause apprehension around the cause-effect issue, perhaps they should be left alone. I feel this is a personal matter. If you, as a parent or teacher, feel uncomfortable with these activities, don't initiate them. Remember, however, that *your children will experience other ways of knowing with or without adult guidance*. The compassionate and understanding adult can not only allay a child's confusion about unusual thought experiences but can also turn such experiences into positive qualities of mindwork.

In the larger picture, honing such ways of knowing might be considered a metaphor for the journeys of discovery embarked upon when humans set out to see the world. What was once terrifying and dreadful has become commonplace and familiar. Tommorrow's children may take mind voyages that today are inconceivable. These will be undertaken without the drugs or external additives in use today. Whether we like it or not, our minds are here, and this era's explorations are expanding the boundaries of yesterday's mind.

Synchronicity: The Times When Things Fit

Synchronicity was popularized by C. G. Jung in his explorations of human consciousness. Synchronicity has to do with harmony. It relates to the bringing together of circumstances and events based on harmony rather than accident. Another word that has been used to mean synchronicity is, in fact, not related at all: coincidence. Coincidence is the random juxtaposition of events in space and time. Synchronicity is the harmonious blending of events in space and time.

Recall Sheldrake's hypothesis of morphogenetic force and morphic resonance. If there is an application here, synchronicity would be an expression of the harmonic patterning of things.

Ask children to remember or write down the times when things work perfectly. This exercise may counteract the countless events that seem to offer the opposite. Be sure to provide pre-writers with a genuine request to be told about the "things that work just right." If this activity begins to shift the children's attention to harmonious experiences and away from failure, it may have served a lifelong purpose.

Many researchers in the area of creativity talk about the way the prepared mind is the most likely to make the discovery or solve the problem. In a way, this activity predisposes the mind to recognize harmony and to blend with that harmony. This predisposition can be taught. Perhaps there is validity to the traditional Hopi saying, "If I go into the world and seek evil, all I will see is evil. If I go into the world seeking goodness then all I will see is goodness. If I choose to have goodness in my heart then I add to the goodness of the world."

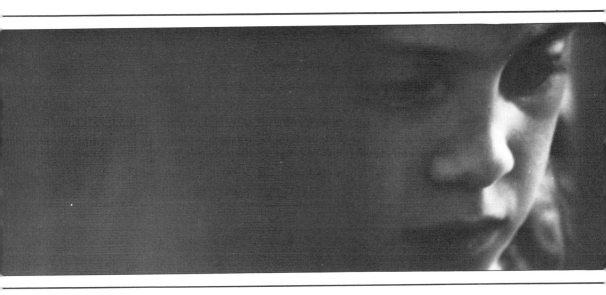

We have created self-im-
posed limitations which are
likely to impair our abilities to
survive with grace, peace
and health in the future.

The Promise of Mind

A story has been told about how Inuit hunters, the people we call Eskimo, take action when they have been unsuccessful for a long time. This measure comes only after their search for caribou has resulted in repeated failure. A person of power, perhaps a shaman, brings forth a dried and protected scapula, the shoulder blade of a caribou taken on an earlier hunt. A fire is built and the scapula is heated almost to the kindling point. The bone is then taken and laid upon the snow where the temperature shock causes it to crack and splinter. The person of power then studies the lines on the broken bone and uses them to guide the hunters to the next hunting site.

A great deal can be read into the story above, depending on the background and inclinations of the reader. A person trained in anthropology might want the sources of the story and be concerned about its authenticity. A hunter trained in our Western vision of hunting might scoff at the premise of the story and cite the need for good tracking skills or at least a helicopter to locate the game. A member of the clergy might see this as some primitive rite appealing to a pagan God. To a student of the brain-mind system, this story represents an example of how people can offer themselves a ready-made mind shift. The process enhances flexibility and increases options.

Throughout this book we have been exploring how to use the information, examples and activities with our children and our students. But be sure that the flexibility we choose to offer children can benefit us as well. The contents of this book are about mind—the mind that we all possess and frequently share.

Perhaps some readers felt that a more straight-forward and didactic approach was needed. I hoped that whatever structure might be needed would be created by that reader. This writing was intended to be a collection of ingredients; the responsibility for assembling these ingredients and creating a recipe lies with the reader.

If I am to claim a sense of responsibility and a hope for the messages in this book, they would be simply stated as follows. The brain-mind-body system is an open system. It is genetically mandated to be open. The habits which deprive us of this openness are learned and maintained by choice. Personal conviction can and will change these acquired habits. However, they need not be learned in the first place. Parenting and formal schooling can be patterned so as to honor the inherent openness of our brain-mind-body system. This book has shared some guidelines toward that end.

Gregory Bateson was convinced that a system of aesthetics was the primary foundation of nature. He defined aesthetics as the pattern which connects. Reason represented that which was connected. Bateson's challenge to us was to merge science with aesthetics as well as reason. To the reductivist, the specificity and rationality of reason is an end in and of itself. The reductivism of Western thought has prevailed for several centuries. Only in the past hundred years have we begun to acknowledge the urges to re-discover the aesthetic. A whole mind includes aesthetics and reason.

Once the mind caresses itself into expression, we hear the completeness of its melodies, the depth of its tone and the integrity of its harmony. To ourselves we owe the richest kind of artistry in the access and expression of our minds. We owe to ourselves the reality of knowing that the process of learning and the experience of excellence are lifelong adventures. We owe to our children the freedom to gain the friendship of their minds—to know that this friend will accompany them with the most lofty loyalty throughout their lives. We owe to the children in our homes and schools a supporting context of wholeness and unity. Homes and schools should be cathedrals of fulfillment, where success is measured by the completeness and richness of human experience rather than the bitter arrogance of narrowness.

If we speak of axial periods in human history, this is the threshold.
Elise Boulding

Mind is the child of the universe. It is the medium that provides the experience and understanding that all beings share. It is the web of consciousness, enchantment and reason. When we begin to honor the possibilities imbedded within its design, we will again embark toward unity. The promise of mind is you and the promise of mind is today.

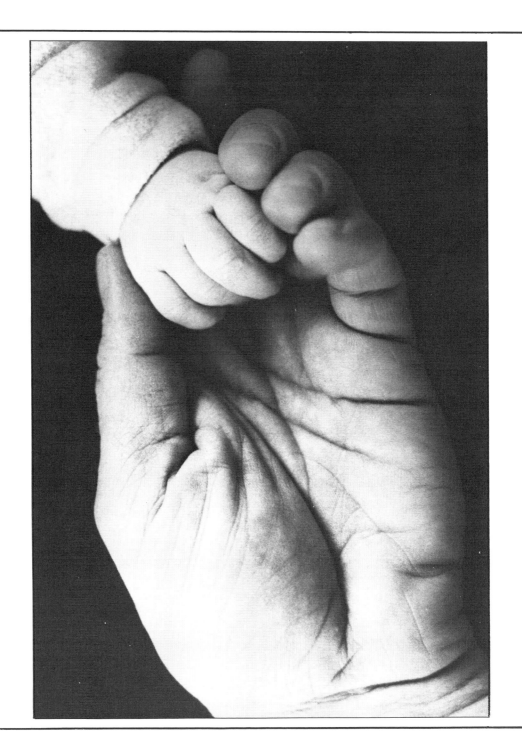

Notes

1. Robert Rivlin and Karen Gravelle, *Deciphering the Senses* (New York: Simon and Schuster, 1984).

2. David B. Guralnik, Ed., *Webster's New World Dictionary of the American Language* (New York: World Publishing, 1972), p. 171.

3. Jess Stein, Ed., *The Random House Dictionary of the English Language* (New York: Random House, 1981), p. 911.

4. Colin Turnbull, *The Human Cycle* (New York: Simon and Schuster, 1983), p. 15.

Bibliography

Bateson, Gregory. *Mind and Nature: A Necessary Unity.* New York: E.P. Dutton, 1979.

Bateson, Mary Catherine. *With a Daughter's Eye: A Memoir of Margaret Mead and Gregory Bateson.* New York: William Morrow and Company, 1984.

Bogen, Joseph E. "The Other Side of the Brain: An Appositional Mind." *Bulletin of the Los Angeles Neurological Societies* 34 (July, 1969).

Bruner, Jerome S. *On Knowing: Essays for the Left Hand.* New York: Atheneum, 1973.

Bruner, Jerome S. *Actual Minds, Possible Worlds.* Cambridge, MA: Harvard University Press, 1986.

Capra, Fritjof. *The Turning Point: Science, Society and the Rising Culture.* New York: Bantam Books, 1983.

Cobb, Edith. *The Ecology of Imagination in Childhood.* New York: Columbia University Press, 1977.

Deloria, Vine, Jr. *The Metaphysics of Modern Existence.* New York: Harper and Row, 1979.

Dewey, John. *John Dewey on Education: Selected Writings.* New York: Random House, 1964.

Donaldson, Margaret. *Children's Minds.* Glasgow: William Collins Sons, 1978.

Eccles, John C., Sir; and Daniel N. Robinson. *The Wonder of Being Human: Our Brain and Our Mind.* Boston: Shambhala Publications, New Science Library, 1984.

Einstein, Albert. *Ideas and Opinions.* New York: Dell, 1973.

Ferguson, Marilyn. *The Aquarian Conspiracy.* Los Angeles: Tarcher, 1980.

Fuller, R. Buckminster. *Synergetics: Explorations in the Geometry of Thinking.* New York: Macmillan, 1975.

Fuller, R. Buckminster. *Synergetics 2: Explorations in the Geometry of Thinking.* New York: Macmillan, 1979.

Galin, David; and Robert Ornstein. "Lateral Specialization of the Cognitive Mode: An EEG Study." *Psychophysiology* 9 (1972).

Gardner, Howard. *Frames of Mind: The Theory of Multiple Intelligences.* New York: Basic Books, 1983.

Hart, Leslie. *How the Brain Works*. New York: Basic Books, 1975.

Highwater, Jamake. *The Primal Mind: Vision and Ritual in Indian America*. New York: Harper and Row, 1981.

Jantsch, Erich. *The Self-Organizing Universe: Scientific and Human Implications of the Emerging Paradigm of Evolution*. New York: Pergamon Press, 1980.

Johnson, David W.; Roger T. Johnson; and Edythe Johnson Holubec. *Cycles of Learning: Cooperation in the Classroom*. Edina, MN: Interaction Book Co., 1986.

Jones, Richard M. *Fantasy and Feeling in Education*. New York: New York University Press, 1968.

Jones, Richard M. *The New Psychology of Dreaming*. New York: Grune and Stratton, 1970.

Kolb, David A. *Organizational Psychology: An Experiential Approach*. Third edition. Englewood Cliffs, NJ: Prentice Hall, 1979.

Kubie, Lawrence S. *Neurotic Distortion of the Creative Process*. Lawrence, KS: University of Kansas Press, 1958.

Leonard, George B. *The Transformation: A Guide to the Inevitable Changes in Humankind*. New York: Delacorte Press, 1972.

McCarthy, Bernice. *The 4MAT System: Teaching to Learning Styles with Right/Left Mode Techniques*. Barrington, IL: Excel, 1981.

Mead, Margaret. *The School in American Culture*. Cambridge, MA: Harvard University Press, 1951.

Pribram, Karl. *Languages of the Brain*. Englewood Cliffs, NJ: Prentice Hall, 1971.

Rivlin, Robert; and Karen Gravelle. *Deciphering the Senses*. New York: Simon and Schuster, 1984.

Samples, Bob. *The Metaphoric Mind: A Celebration of Creative Consciousness*. Second edition. Rolling Hills Estates, CA: Jalmar Press, in press.

Sheldrake, Rupert. *A New Science of Life: The Hypothesis of Formative Causation*. Los Angeles: Tarcher, 1981.

Sternberg, Robert J. *Beyond IQ: A Triarchic Theory of Intelligence*. Cambridge, U.K.: Cambridge University Press, 1985.

Turnbull, Colin. *The Human Cycle*. New York: Simon and Schuster, 1983.

Acknowledgements

This book is a chronicle of cooperation brought about by hundreds of visitors to my consciousness. Some are listed below and some have slipped beyond my mind's ability to remember.

To a Context:
Gold Hill, Colorado is a place of love, fear, competition, arrogance, joy, cooperation, pride, compassion and competence—in other words, a place to live and grow. Thanks to it and to our choice to be part of it.

Ideamakers and Friends:
Jerome Bruner, Richard Jones, Margaret Donaldson, Eleanor Duckworth, R. Buckminster Fuller, Ned Herrmann, Milton McClaren, Bernice McCarthy, David Kolb, Dorothy Sherman, William J.J. Gordon, Bob Burden, Fritjof Capra, Carl Rogers, Gregory Bateson, Ted Roszak, Vine Deloria, Jamake Highwater, O.J. Harvey, Willi Unsoeld, Karl Pribram, Leslie Hart, Joseph Bogen, Larry Kubie, David Galin, Jean Houston, Marilyn Ferguson, John Denver, Willis Harman, George Leonard, Tony Buzan, Dee Dickinson, Hazel Henderson, Jonas Salk, Tom Crum, Jean-Michel Cousteau, Bob Sillwester, Mike Hartoonian, Tony Angell.

If there is confirming resonance within us, it may be because our lives have overlapped with those we encounter.
Theodore Roszak

Teachers of the Precious Sort:
Steven Vanek, Pat McQuown, Anne Snow, Mathew Morrison, Pat Manka, Marie Brookhart, Holly Huth, Lynn Wolf.

More Teachers and Friends:
Ken Peterson, Sue Miller, Bill Hammond, Annie Watson, Helen Musselman, Jack Henes, Robbie Porter, Jake Nice, John Thompson, Barbara Meister-Vitale, Kerry Baldwin, Roger Johnson, Frank Watson, Tom Charles, Rene Shelver, Jim Gladson, Vickie Vandever, Don Green, Harry Zimbrick, Warren Dohman, Jim Leary, Tilford Jackson, Si King, Tom Evans, Maurice Gibbons, Susan Leflar, Sr. Marian Walsh, Paul Dolan, Calvin Taylor.

Those who helped:
Judy Dawson, Linda Haschke, Suzanne Mikesell, Brad Winch.

And one who for me is all the above:
Cheryl Charles.

About the Author

Bob Samples is an independent scholar whose work takes him throughout the world lecturing and conducting workshops in education, creativity, brain-mind design, personality/stress and systems theory. Author of six books including the classic *Metaphoric Mind*, Samples focuses on the design of the brain-mind system and how cultural systems have come to inhibit natural capabilities in human learning and management. Both his writing and film work have won national awards. Originally trained in the physical sciences of geology and astronomy, Samples was drawn into education and psychology when invited to contribute to science curriculum projects funded by the National Science Foundation in the early 1960s. Since that time, he has explored both the breadth and continuity of learning throughout life.

Correspondence to Bob Samples should be addressed to:
Hawksong
P.O. Box 18060
Boulder, CO 80308-8060